ON THE PATH
OF VENUS

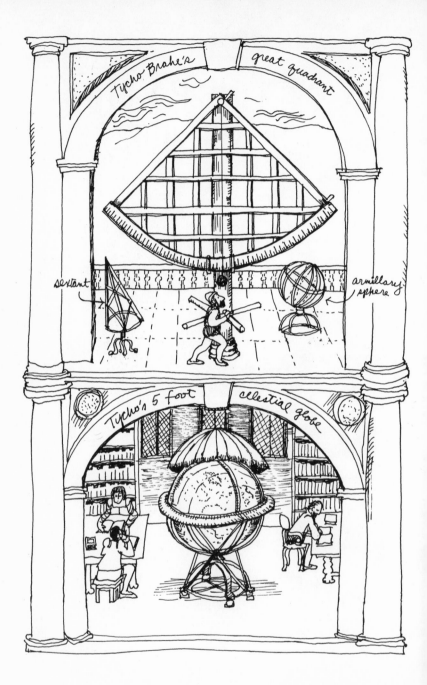

Tycho Brahe's great quadrant

sextant

armillary sphere

Tycho's 5 foot celestial globe

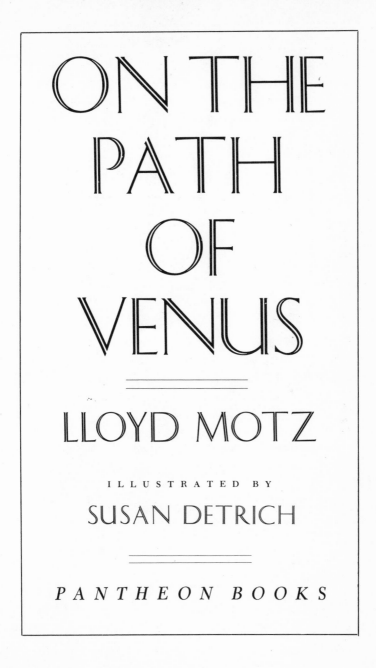

ON THE PATH OF VENUS

LLOYD MOTZ

ILLUSTRATED BY

SUSAN DETRICH

PANTHEON BOOKS

Library of Congress Cataloging in Publication Data

Motz, Lloyd, 1910–   On the path of Venus.

SUMMARY: Traces the development of man's understanding of the solar system

by examining the contributions of astronomers through the ages

whose curiosity was aroused by the planet Venus.

1. Solar system—Juvenile literature. 2. Astronomy—History—Juvenile literature.

[1. Venus (Planet) 2. Solar system 3. Astronomers]   I. Detrich, Susan,   II. Title.

QB501.3.M67   523.2   75-45415

ISBN 0–394–83106–3

ISBN 0–394–93106–8 lib. bdg.

Manufactured in the United States of America

10 9 8 7 6 5 4 3 2 1

TO MINNE, ROBIN, AND JULIE

CONTENTS

ON THE PATH
OF VENUS

⊢IN THE LIBRARY

The room was cool and quiet, the way Michael liked it, and the slanting rays of the setting sun cast a strange glow on the shelves of books that covered three of the walls from floor to ceiling. Michael had always felt drawn to these books, and his desire to be able to read and understand them was so intense it was almost like being hungry. Their very titles—*Celestial Mechanics, Thermodynamics, Cosmology, Astrophysics*—were strange-sounding and intrigued Michael. Sitting in the deep leather chair, he studied the books and wondered about the authors and how they had come to write them.

He recognized some of the names—like Newton, Einstein, and Fermi—people he had read a great deal about, and he noted, with pride, that his father's name appeared on some of the books on astrophysics. He knew that the books described wonderful scientific discoveries in the language scientists themselves used, and he sometimes wondered if he would ever know enough to understand this language and do scientific research himself. How young were these famous scientists when they began making their discoveries? Were any of them as young as he was now, he wondered?

When Michael first thought about becoming a scientist, he wasn't exactly sure what scientists did, even though his father was one. As far as Michael could see his father spent a lot of time sitting at his desk either reading books and science journals or covering page upon page of notebooks with mathematical symbols. It seemed a mystery that anyone could discover the secrets of nature this way. But Michael knew he was interested in the very things his father was.

As far back as Michael could remember he had wondered about the stars and the planets. He would never forget the first time he looked through a telescope. He had decided then that he would study astronomy. There were so many riddles to be solved in astronomy, and there would still be some left for him when he became an astronomer.

Michael had read everything he could find about the planets in his father's library. Each one gave him something strange and wonderful to think about. Saturn, by far the most beautiful when seen through a telescope, had its amazing rings which astronomers said consist of lumps of matter whirling around it. It was believed that at one time—a very long time ago—these lumps were collected together into a moon of Saturn's that had wandered too close to the planet and had been ripped into bits by Saturn's gravity. Saturn was very large, and very massive, but gallon for gallon it was not even as heavy as water. Saturn could actually float in water if there were an ocean large enough to hold it. Astronomers had figured this out, using the kind of mathematics Michael's father worked with.

Then there was Jupiter, the most massive and largest of the planets, with its thirteen moons, four of which were first discovered by Galileo hundreds of years ago. He was the first man to look at the planets through a telescope— a telescope he had built himself. Jupiter was so massive that a person standing on its surface would weigh almost three times as much as he weighs on earth and would almost be squashed by his own weight. But nobody really knew how deep down below Jupiter's atmosphere Jupiter's surface began or what it was like. Perhaps it was all ice or liquid ammonia or liquid hydrogen. Long before an astronaut felt his feet hit solid ground on Jupiter, he would be frozen stiffer than an icicle. Michael shivered slightly at the thought. What a strange planet Jupiter was. Some astronomers said it barely missed being a star (a hot body like the sun) and would now *be* a star if it were two or three times more massive than it was. Also very strange was Jupiter's great red spot. It had suddenly appeared about a hundred years ago and had been puzzling astronomers ever since. The red spot was almost four times larger than the earth and floated around at the top of Jupiter's atmosphere like a huge glacier in an ocean, hardly changing from year to year.

Michael's thoughts shifted to Mars, the planet that

always looked red as it was rising. The ancients named Mars after the god of war because its color reminded them of blood, though it didn't look as red as all that. Michael was interested in the idea that there was a time when people thought of the planets as gods; but even today, when everybody spoke of the space age, most people knew very little about the planets.

Michael had spent many hours reading and thinking about Mars because it was generally believed that there was some kind of life on it. The colors on its surface changed from green to brown from time to time as though plants were changing their colors with the seasons. But now that space probes from the earth had come close to Mars and taken pictures of its surface, it didn't look as though there was any life on the planet. Its surface looked very much like the surface of the moon. On learning this, Michael's interest had waned.

His thoughts these days were now almost entirely devoted to Venus—the most mysterious and challenging of all the planets. He had watched Venus in the early morning before the sun rose, when it is sometimes called the morning star, and in the early evening after the sun had set, when it is called the evening star. How many people in the past had watched it as he did and had marveled at it, wondering what kind of object it was? It was so brilliant in the sky that it made you wonder. Even the best and largest telescopes revealed very little about Venus because of the dense, opaque cloud that surrounds it. Nobody even knew what the cloud was made of. Michael knew that Venus was about as large and as massive as the earth. He had hoped, when he had first read about Venus, that its surface might be like the earth's surface, with beautiful rivers, mountains, and valleys. But now he knew that astronomers had found, by studying the radio waves that come from the surface of Venus, that it is very much hotter than the earth—far too hot for rivers and trees.

When Michael first heard this, he was puzzled. What do radio waves have to do with heat? How does Venus manage to send out waves that show how hot it is? Michael decided to ask his father. He knew he wouldn't get a direct answer from him—he never did. His father had a way of *answering* Michael's questions by *asking* him questions. His father would throw questions at him quite casually. They seemed very simple at first, but as Michael thought about them and tried to answer them, he saw how carefully thought-out they were and that each question taught him something new, until finally the whole thing appeared very clear and he had arrived at the answer to the question he had asked in the first place.

When Michael asked about the radio waves from the surface of Venus, his father did not answer in his usual way but began talking about the way Venus appeared to the ancient Greeks, the ancient Egyptians, and the other peoples who lived thousands of years ago. He hinted at the many exciting stories about the growth of astronomy from the very simple ideas of those early people to the very complicated theories that are now accepted.

He never did answer Michael's question; but one day, a few weeks later, Michael noticed a neatly bound sheaf of papers on his father's desk. He knew that this generally meant his father was writing a scientific paper, so he walked over to read the title, and was surprised to see the words ON THE PATH OF VENUS: *Written for Michael* on the cover page. He turned to the first story . . . in a few minutes he was back in the past, some two thousand years ago, on a small Grecian island.

2 - VENUS AND THE GREEK BOY OF SAMOS

Just after sunset one early spring evening many, many years ago, a small, dark-haired boy, hardly twelve years old, was watching the western sky intently. He was sitting on a hill at the southern tip of the Greek island of Samos, where he lived with his shepherd father, his mother, and a younger sister. A few hundred feet below him the rough waters of the Aegean Sea pounded the huge rocks and boulders that were piled up along the shore as though cast up from the ocean floor by some angry sea monster. Aristar, for that was the Greek boy's name, loved to watch the waves break against the rocks and boil into white foam, but on this evening the rocks and waves were forgotten. His entire attention was directed to the small patch of sky above the western horizon where the sun had just set. He was very excited and in a state of great expectation because a remarkable idea of his was about to be proved or disproved. He

7

expected a certain bright object to appear near the point in the sky he was watching. If it did appear soon, and he was sure it would, all his calculations would be proved right. He felt like an explorer who was about to see the shores of a new continent emerge from the distant seas.

From his perch above the waters, Aristar could see to the east the land now known as Turkey; but then, about three hundred years before the birth of Christ, the Greeks called it Byzantium. It was a mysterious land about which many fables had been written, and storytellers said that the sun was a god that lived there during the night in a magnificent palace. Aristar did not believe that, nor did he believe any of the fables that linked the stellar constellations and the planets to the gods and the Greek heroes. He was a strange, thoughtful lad who disturbed his playmates and his parents as much by his long periods of silence as by what he said. He had been told over and over again that he was offending the gods and would one day bring destruction on himself and his home, but he could no more stop thinking and acting as he did than he could stop breathing.

It had all begun about a year earlier. One morning his father had awakened him before sunrise and had brought him to this same spot to help tend their sheep. This was the first time in his life that Aristar had seen the early morning sky, and he marveled at its beauty. But he was also puzzled by it, for he saw none of the stars that were in the sky when he had gone to bed the night before. Everything was different—even the Milky Way. Where were the stars of the night before, and how had they been replaced overnight by these new ones? Even as he wondered about this and looked at what at first appeared to be a group of unfamiliar stars and constellations, he saw that they were not really strangers to him. They were the very stars and constellations he had seen in the night sky after sunset last autumn. That exciting discovery gave him the answer to his question. The same stars are always in the sky, but not all of them can be seen at the same time because they are spread out all around the sky. Only half the stars were in the half of the sky that he saw above him on that morning just before dawn. The other half, the stars that he had seen the night before, had already set and were below the horizon. Six months later, in autumn, these same stars and constellations would again be in the sky after sunset; and the stars he saw last night before going to bed would then be visible before sunrise. The stars that were visible after sunrise in the winter months would be visible before sunrise in the summer months.

These thoughts had hardly passed through Aristar's mind that morning when he was startled by the sudden appearance of a gloriously bright object in the eastern sky, right above the mysterious land of Byzantium. Struck by its great beauty, he just stood there staring at it. At first he thought it was an unusually bright star, but he soon gave up that idea. If it were a star, it would belong to one of the visible constellations, and he would then have seen it in that constellation last fall when these same stars were in the early evening sky right after sunset. But he had never seen this object before. Anyway, all the stars he had ever seen never stopped twinkling; this brilliant body, unlike the stars, didn't twinkle at all. It just rose higher and higher in the sky, sending its steady untwinkling rays of light to earth. Pointing to this bright heavenly body, Aristar asked his father about it and was told that it was called *Phosphorus*, the morning star. This was the very object that we call *Venus* today—one of the nine planets.

The boy bubbled over with questions, but his father could tell him no more about the morning star than the name the Greeks had given it and that it was called a *planet*, which is the Greek word for "wanderer" because, unlike the stars which occupy fixed positions in the constellations, it shifts its position relative to the stars and moves from constellation to constellation during the year.

Aristar could not take his eyes from Phosphorus. But even as he felt himself drawn more and more to it, the morning star faded away as the first brilliant rays of the rising sun bathed all the land, sky, and water around him in light. He stood there for a moment noting, just before Phosphorus disappeared, that if he stretched his right arm out as far as he could, he could lay off the palm of his hand four times on the sky between the rising sun and fading Phosphorus. In doing this Aristar had made his first astronomical measurement. He explained to his father that by doing this each morning at sunrise he could discover precisely how Phosphorus moved across the sky. Being a loving parent, Aristar's father agreed to bring the boy to that same spot every morning and allow him to study the daily movement of the morning star.

Phosphorus
(Venus)
as a morning star in its
westward motion away
from the sun)

the rising
sun

Horizon

east

west

Aristar
estimating the angular separation of
Venus from the sun in the early morning.

Something about the stars, some mystery, had drawn Aristar as a magnet draws iron. He had constantly asked questions about the heavenly bodies that no one could answer; he had decided, when he was no more than eight years old, to find things out for himself. Now, at the age of twelve, he was going to unravel the mystery of Phosphorus, the morning star. Morning after morning Aristar followed his father to the herd of sheep, and each morning he watched Phosphorus rise and then counted the number of times he could lay off the palm of his outstretched hand on the sky between Phosphorus and the rising sun. He soon discovered that Phosphorus rose a bit earlier each morning because it moved away from the sun westward by a small amount each day. Using his extended arm he discovered that every four or five days the wanderer Phosphorus moved away from the sun by an amount on the sky just about equal to the width of the palm of his extended hand. He did not know why this happened, but just discovering it and knowing that it did move that way made him very happy.

As the days wore on and spring began to give way to summer, the time between the rising of Phosphorus and sunrise increased steadily. Finally, about eighteen days before the first day of summer, Phosphorus rose more than three hours before sunrise, and Aristar found that his palm, when his arm was fully extended, could be laid off about sixteen times between Phosphorus and the point on the eastern horizon where the sun was just beginning to appear. On that particular day the beautiful wanderer

Phosphorus was among the stars in the constellation Aquarius, the water carrier.

When Aristar went to bed that night, he wondered whether Phosphorus would continue moving westward away from the sun as it had been doing since the morning he first saw it. He suspected it would not, for he had noted that it had slowed down in its westward motion during the last few days. He was sure it would stop altogether and begin to approach the sun again. This was such an exciting idea that he could hardly sleep. He kept wondering about the planet and why it moved in such a strange manner. The next few mornings proved him right, for Phosphorus stopped moving westward and began to move eastward toward the sun. But its eastward motion toward the sun was much slower than its westward motion away from it had been. Aristar had to wait more than half a year before Phosphorus had come so close to the sun that he could no longer see it in the early morning before the sun rose. By that time winter had come, and the sky looked quite different. The days were short and the nights were long.

He was glad now that he could no longer see Phosphorus before sunrise because it was too cold to get out of bed. But much as he loved to lie under the warm covers on those cold winter mornings, he would have forced himself to jump out and study the wanderer if it could still be seen. As he lay under the warm covers one morning, listening to his mother moving about in the kitchen, his mind was torn between two pleasures. Either

13

to think of the mysterious wanderings of Phosphorus or to contemplate the warm, crisp bread covered with sweet fresh butter and thick slices of goat's cheese that his mother was preparing for breakfast. He could hear the logs burning in the fireplace in the kitchen, and he knew that his mother was warming milk for him to drink with his bread and cheese.

He thought of his mother now. As far back as he could remember, she had encouraged him as he told her his strange thoughts. When other adults frowned at what he said, she smiled at him with such tender love and her face became so radiant that he wanted her to look like that forever.

This jumble of ideas filled Aristar's mind for only a few minutes before he dismissed it and turned his thoughts to his beloved Phosphorus. He had discovered a pattern in its motion away from and toward the sun. He now knew that Phosphorus must have been very close to the sun for a number of days before he had discovered it that early spring morning when he had first gone with his father to tend the sheep. It rose and set with the sun during those earlier days and so could not be seen, but little by little it drew away from the sun westward until it could be seen rising by itself. Aristar estimated that it spent about seventy-two days moving away from the sun before it turned back and began to move toward the sun again, which it did just before summer began. He had then made the remarkable discovery that it would take Phosphorus 220 days to return to the neighborhood of the sun again, where it now was, during these wintry days.

As he thought about these things, another idea struck him. Phosphorus would not stop at the sun but would continue moving eastward right past the sun. It would then rise after sunset. That meant he should be able to see it again in a few more weeks, but this time in the early evening, shortly after sunset, instead of in the early mornings before dawn. It all fit together beautifully. Which brings us back to the beginning of our story and to the early spring evening when Aristar was perched above the Aegean Sea, intently watching the western sky.

Weeks before, he had figured out from earlier observations that Phosphorus would be far enough to the east of the sun on this very day to be visible above the western horizon for about half an hour after the sun had set. Although he did not have the slightest doubt that he would see Phosphorus just where he had estimated it would be that evening, he was still so excited that his eyes played tricks on him, and he imagined he saw it a few times before he actually did see it. Then suddenly it was there, faint in the twilight rays of the sun, but unmistakable. He had been right. Phosphorus was right on time, exactly where he had expected it to be. But before he had a chance to call his mother and father and tell them of his great discovery, the planet sank below the horizon.

That night at supper he was so restless and talked so much and so rapidly that hardly anyone else could get a word in. Wanting to surprise his parents with his discovery next evening, he did not tell what he had seen. He merely hinted at some great marvel that had befallen

Hesperus (Venus as an evening star) receding from the Sun eastwardly.

Horizon

East

We[st]

Aristar observing Venus in the early evening.

him. Aristar's father quieted him down a few times, but his mother encouraged him with her gentle eyes and sweet smile. She knew him well enough to understand that behind his excitement lay something very important. As the evening wore on, she became almost as excited as Aristar and wondered what his secret was. He finally gave them a clue by asking them to watch the early evening sky with him tomorrow.

The next evening, right after sunset, the whole family was standing where Aristar had sat twenty-four hours earlier, watching the sky above the spot on the western horizon where the sun had just set. Suddenly Aristar's sister called out excitedly, "I see something, I see something—I see the first star of the night." They all saw it! Then Aristar boldly announced that it was not a star at all but the planet Phosphorus.

His father looked at him curiously and said quietly, with some disappointment in his words, "You are wrong, Aristar. It is not Phosphorus; it is the evening star. It is the wanderer Hesperus that is reborn every time Phosphorus dies. And Phosphorus is reborn when Hesperus dies."

Aristar, seeing his mother's questioning face, explained carefully how he had followed the motion of Phosphorus in its eastward and westward wanderings during the year and had predicted its reappearance in the evening sky. He saw that his mother understood him and accepted his explanation, but his father was puzzled. Speaking very carefully, Aristar explained that Phosphorus and Hesperus were merely different names for the same planet seen at different times of the day. Phosphorus, or Hesperus, would continue moving away from the sun in an eastward direction for 220 more days. At the end of that time the planet would be visible in the evening for about three hours after the sun had set, and the palm of his extended hand would then fit about sixteen times in the space on the sky between Phosphorus and the sun.

Aristar's father interrupted him with questions now and then, but as Aristar answered these without hesitation, his father became convinced that the boy was right. He marveled that one so young could make such important discoveries. People had always thought that Hesperus and Phosphorus were different planets; now this lad, his own son, had proved them wrong. He suddenly felt very proud, and the radiant face of his wife told him she felt as he did.

But Aristar had not yet finished. He went on to say that after withdrawing eastward from the sun for 220 days, Phosphorus would stop moving eastward and would begin moving westward toward the sun again. It would reach the sun in its westward motion in 72 days, pass it, and appear again in the early morning sky as the morning star. From then on it would draw away from the sun in a westerly direction for 72 more days. It would then start all over again in its eastward motion, first approaching the sun for 220 days and then drawing away from it in an easterly direction for another 220 days. Aristar told his family that he had figured the whole thing out very carefully. Phosphorus, or Hesperus, swings from one side of the sun to the other and back again every 584 days. It spends 144 days moving westward from constellation to constellation, and 440 days moving eastward.

All this came to pass in time as Aristar had predicted, and his fame spread throughout Greece and even beyond. He came to be known as the wonder child. Learned men came from all over, even from the mysterious land to the east, to question him about his discoveries.

As Aristar grew into manhood, he discovered so many important things about the sun, the moon, the planets, and the stars that he came to be known as Aristarchus of Samos—the wisest man in all Greece. Hardly a day passed that people did not come to listen to him and write down all he said. To these people he gave whatever knowledge he had, but not everybody could understand him for he spoke about many complicated things. Aristarchus did not agree with the accepted idea at that time that the earth was fixed at the center of the universe and that the entire sky, with the stars, sun, and planets, revolved around it. After countless nights of studying the stars and the planets and observing carefully the changes in the sky from season to season, he was led to the belief that the sun and the stars are fixed and that the earth moves. The sun and the stars only appear to move.

He told those who listened to him that the stars and all the other heavenly bodies such as the sun, the moon, and the planets appear to rise in the east and set in the west every day because the earth itself turns every day from west to east like a huge top. This makes the sky appear to turn from east to west. Not only is the earth spinning, he said; it is also moving in a vast circle around the sun, like a stone in a twirling sling. Because the earth moves around the sun by a small amount each day, said Aristarchus, the sun itself appears to shift slightly to the east among the stars each day. That is why the stars rise a bit earlier each day and why every six months the early morning stars become the evening stars and the evening stars become early morning stars. The stars that we can see any evening are those that lie in that part of the sky which is opposite to where the sun appears to lie.

Aristarchus had figured this out about a dozen years after he had first seen Phosphorus. After solving the puzzle of Phosphorus and Hesperus, he studied the motions of the other planets; night after night he thought about the changing appearance of the sky. Before falling asleep, he imagined himself far away among the stars, watching the earth, the sun, the moon, and the planets. But he was always fast asleep before he could do much thinking. And so it went on for some time. One night, the answer came to him quite suddenly, and he was amazed at how simple it was. Everything could be explained if the earth was not fixed but was moving around a fixed sun. He saw that because people living on the earth could not feel the earth's motion, they would insist that the earth was fixed, as they had always thought it to be.

He told no one about this startling idea of his, except his mother. She was shocked and somewhat frightened because she was sure the gods would be offended by such strange beliefs and would punish Aristarchus. But he explained everything in such a clear and simple way and gave such strong reasons for his ideas that she had to believe him. Her son was a grown man now, taller than his father—and more handsome, she thought. But he had lost none of the wonder about nature that had stirred him as a boy. He had become everything she had hoped for—a wise and gentle person, a great teacher, and a lover of wisdom and knowledge. The gods had been kind to her to give her a son who could understand and explain the mysteries of the universe.

That the earth is not fixed but revolves around the sun had come to Aristarchus easily enough. But he knew that such an idea would not be accepted unless he had some kind of proof for it. Although he never could prove his theory, he finally found what he thought was very strong evidence in its favor. By carefully observing the angle formed by the directions of the moon and sun from the earth when the moon is exactly half lit up (what we call half moon) and noting that this angle was almost 90 degrees, he found that the sun's distance from the earth is many times greater than the moon's distance from the earth. If the distances of the moon and sun were almost the same, the angle would be about 45 degrees. Knowing that the moon and the sun appear to be of the same size, he reasoned from this that the sun must be many times larger than the moon and, therefore, many times larger than the earth which he knew, from lunar eclipses, to be not much larger than the moon. That one fact convinced him that the sun is fixed and the earth is revolving around the sun. He thought it unreasonable to have a very large body like the sun revolve around a much smaller one like the earth.

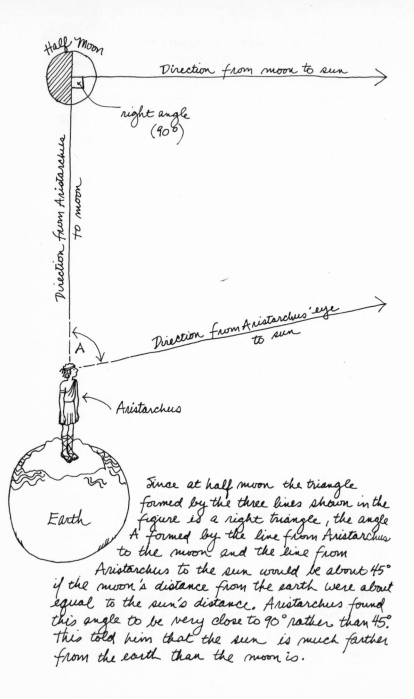

Half Moon

Direction from moon to sun

right angle
(90°)

Direction from Aristarchus to moon

Direction from Aristarchus' eye to sun

A

Aristarchus

Earth

Since at half moon the triangle
formed by the three lines shown in the
figure is a right triangle, the angle
A formed by the line from Aristarchus
to the moon and the line from
Aristarchus to the sun would be about 45°
if the moon's distance from the earth were about
equal to the sun's distance. Aristarchus found
this angle to be very close to 90° rather than 45°.
This told him that the sun is much farther
from the earth than the moon is.

It did not take Aristarchus long to go from the idea of a revolving earth to revolving planets. He imagined the sun to be the ruler of a solar system that commanded not only the earth but all the other planets as well, forcing them to move around it in circles. He did not know how the sun did this, but he did not worry too much about that. Believing that the earth moves around the sun once a year, and knowing that Phosphorus appears to swing back and forth from one side of the sun to the other once every 584 days, about 48 degrees to either side of the sun, he figured out that Phosphorus revolves around the sun once every 225 days in a smaller circle than the earth's circle around the sun. This explained why Phosphorus always appears to swing from one side of the sun to the other. Its circle lies within the earth's circle. If its orbit were larger than the earth's orbit, Venus would sometimes appear in a direction at right angles to the sun's direction, and sometimes it would appear to rise when the sun is setting; but this never happens.

Later in his life he studied the planet Mercury and saw that Mercury behaves like Phosphorus, except that it moves back and forth, from side to side of the sun, more rapidly. From this he reasoned that Mercury revolves around the sun in a circle that is smaller than the circle of Phosphorus and much smaller than the earth's circle.

Aristarchus also studied the planets Mars, Jupiter, and Saturn, which do not appear to swing from side to side of the sun but appear to move in loops from one constellation to another. After much thought, he saw that the looping motions of these three planets could also be explained if they were moving around the sun in circles that were larger than the earth's circle. Everything fit together so beautifully that Aristarchus was sure he was right, as we now know he was.

But people forgot what he said and what was written down in those long ago days, and they went back to believing that the earth is fixed at the center of the universe and that the sky really turns around the earth. They believed this for almost two thousand years after Aristarchus lived. But what the boy Aristar began when he first studied the motion of Phosphorus, and the beautiful picture of the solar system that Aristarchus painted, were never really lost. They were only put aside until another great and wise man saw the truth of the Greek boy's wisdom and rediscovered it, many years after the death of Aristarchus.

Aristarchus did not know what the planet Phosphorus was like, but with his wisdom he probably had a pretty good notion. Knowing that the planets and the earth move around the sun, it was an easy matter for him to believe that Phosphorus, like each of the other planets, was a body like the earth, shining by the reflected light of the sun.

Aristarchus lived to be an old man and was honored by many princes and kings. But wherever he went, he was never as happy as when he was sitting at the tip of the Island of Samos, watching the sun go down into the Aegean Sea and the sky become a carpet of stars.

When Michael finished reading the story of Aristarchus of Samos, he leaned back in his chair, closed his eyes, and pictured himself on the Island of Samos, watching the western sky as he listened to the waves below. He was happy at the idea that had he lived then, he might have done what Aristar did. He had, in fact, observed Venus many times, and he had noted the way it shifted in the sky from one constellation to the next. Just a year ago, when Venus was farthest from the sun to the west, he had even taken a sky chart, showing all the constellations, and had marked the position of Venus on it from week to week. What he had done was very easy compared to Aristar's achievement. There were no sky maps in those days, and nothing like pencil and paper.

Michael was suddenly struck by a thought that bothered him. If Aristarchus was the first to propose the idea that the sun is at the center of the solar system and that the earth and all the other planets revolve around it, why didn't the books Michael had read say so? Why was all the credit given to Copernicus? Michael wondered how and why people had forgotten the work of Aristarchus. What had happened between the death of Aristarchus and the birth of Copernicus to make people forget what Aristarchus had done? With these questions pursuing each other in his mind, he turned to the next chapter of his father's manuscript.

3-CLAUDIUS PTOLEMY: THE GREAT ASTRONOMER OF ALEXANDRIA

The sun had set below the western desert, and the camels, loaded with huge bundles, were slowing down as though they knew that the time to rest had come. Young Claudius Ptolemy and his father had been traveling southward for the last few days, along the western bank of one of the channels of the great Nile River, which the people called the River of Life. They had left the magnificent Egyptian city of Alexandria on the Mediterranean Sea five days ago, and were now approaching the southern end of the vast delta of the Nile. Here the river, which begins as a small headstream 4200 miles to the south, in a remote part of Africa, breaks up into seven channels which thread their way through the rich, fertile soil of the delta and empty into the sea.

Claudius, his father, and their company of servants and porters traveled during the day and rested at night. As soon as the sun set each day, and the first stars were faintly visible, the porters lowered their equipment from the backs of the lumbering camels and began to set up the sleeping tents. Claudius was amazed at how fast they worked and how expertly they constructed each tent. The largest one, in the very center of the camping grounds, was reserved for him and his father. Claudius thought it was quite luxurious. Beautiful furs covered the earthen floor, and the two beds on which he and his father slept were mounds of soft furs covered with silken sheets and woolen blankets. The table at which they were to dine had already been set up. Servants were bringing in plates filled with dates, figs, nuts, and various kinds of sweetmeats.

Claudius, who was then about thirteen years old, had never been far from Alexandria before, and he probably would still have been back there tonight if he hadn't persuaded his father to take him along on this important expedition to the head of the Nile Delta. It was a trip his father took every two years at the bidding of the great Roman emperor Trajan, who ruled Egypt as well as Rome at that time, some 120 years after the birth of Christ. Claudius's father, one of the most learned men in Alexandria, was head of the famous Alexandrian museum which attracted scholars, philosophers, and scientists from every part of the vast Roman Empire. Some came to read and study books, manuscripts, and papyri that had been collected and stored for hundreds of years in the vaults of the museum's library which, in itself, was one of the great wonders of the ancient world. Others came to lecture at the museum, and still others came to pore over the various collections in the museum. Here, among many other things, one could see rocks of all kinds, precious metals, exquisite jewels, hundreds of seashells, astronomical charts, maps, and all kinds of handicraft. Claudius spent most of his idle hours in the museum, making drawings of many of the things he saw and copying from old manuscripts that interested him. He loved astronomical objects and mathematical manuscripts more than any of the other things in the museum. He had already decided that someday he would write books on astronomy and mathematics.

Claudius's parents were born in the small town of Ptolemais in Macedon, which is now known as Macedonia, but which was then a northern province of ancient Greece. He could trace his family back more than four hundred years to the time of Alexander the Great, king of Macedon, conqueror of the whole world and founder of Alexandria. The name Ptolemy was made famous by the Greek dynasty of Ptolemies that ruled Egypt and Alexandria, beginning with Ptolemy I, who was one of Alexander's leading generals, and ending with the beautiful Cleopatra some 150 years before Claudius was born.

Claudius knew that his family was only distantly related to Cleopatra and the royal Ptolemies and counted among its members many famous scholars and writers who had done much to improve the great museum and its libraries. He also knew that his father was quite wealthy, for they lived with many servants on a large estate overlooking the Mediterranean to the north and the valley of the Nile to the south. It was an ideal place from which to observe the heavens; Claudius had spent many hours studying the sky, noting how the constellations that could be seen at night changed from month to month. By the time he was eleven years old, he knew by heart all the constellations and the brighter stars in each constellation, and he could tell at what time of the year each constellation would be visible in the evening sky. Now, at the age of thirteen, he knew from his own observations that each constellation and, in fact, each star rises about four minutes earlier each night. He was very proud of that discovery, which he had made one evening about ten months ago when the dog star Sirius was rising in the east just as the sun, which was in the constellation Capricorn, was setting in the west.

It was unusually clear that late afternoon. Claudius, looking southward, saw the desert to the east of the Nile stretching into the land of Arabia and the vast Sahara Desert lying to the west. He could see the entire horizon from east to west and stood for a moment completely entranced, feeling as though he were the only living being on earth and all this beauty of sky and earth were for him alone. The top rim of the sun had just sunk below the western desert, and as the evening chill settled over him, he saw Sirius just above the eastern desert. Sirius was so bright and the air was so clear that he could see it even though there was still light in the sky; and he wondered at it. He wondered because only fifteen days earlier, when he was standing in the same spot, he had also seen Sirius where it was now—just above the eastern horizon. But that was an hour later than now; the sun was then well below the western horizon, and darkness had already settled over the land. Claudius saw that this meant that Sirius, and therefore all the stars, rose about one hour earlier every fifteen days, or about four minutes earlier each day.

He was so excited by this discovery that he rushed back to his study, where he kept his books, to write down what he had observed. He made careful drawings showing exactly where he was standing that night and fifteen days earlier, and where the sun and Sirius were at those times. While he was doing this he was struck by a remarkable idea which was to guide his thinking about the heavenly bodies for the rest of his life. His idea was that the stars, arranged in unchanging patterns (the constellations), were all fixed on a very distant sphere with the earth at its center. The sun, the moon, and the planets, however, were very much closer to the earth and not fixed to the sphere of stars. The distant stars and, in fact, the entire sky turned around the earth once a day, he reasoned, causing the stars to rise and set. The sun, moon, and planets were also carried around by this daily rotation of the entire sky. But not being rigidly fixed to the distant sphere of stars, the sun, the moon and the planets could shift their positions with respect to the distant stars. Better still, one could picture the sun, moon, and each of the planets carried around the earth, each on its own sphere, with each sphere turning at a different rate.

Those were Claudius Ptolemy's thoughts that early evening so long ago. To explain why all the stars rise about four minutes earlier each day he simply proposed the idea that the sun shifts its position eastward by a small amount each day, or that the sun's sphere turns somewhat more slowly than the stellar sphere. Thus the sun got closer and closer to Sirius's position in the sky each day. In time, the sun and Sirius would rise at the same hour, and Sirius would no longer be visible in the night sky.

As these ideas flashed through his mind, he wrote them down quickly. At the same time he made a rough mental calculation which showed him that in about three months Sirius would be rising at noon, and in about six months it would be rising at sunrise and setting at sunset. After that, Sirius would rise before sunrise and be visible in the early morning sky.

He was elated with these ideas and wondered whether anybody else had made the same discoveries. He didn't have to wonder long. Next day, when he described to his father what he had done, his father said only two words, "Read Hipparchos." Claudius knew what that meant: some manuscripts in the museum's library written by a man named Hipparchos dealt with the very ideas that Claudius had jotted down last night. He could hardly wait to get to those manuscripts.

Claudius was happy that his family had moved to Alexandria and that he had been born there, for it was the most beautiful and exciting city in the world. In the more than four hundred years since it was founded by Alexander the Great, it had grown enormously and had become the cultural center of the world. Here one could

The night sky in spring (on March 21) as it appears to spin around the earth. The planet Venus is shown in the constellation of Aries and the sun is shown in the constellation Pisces.

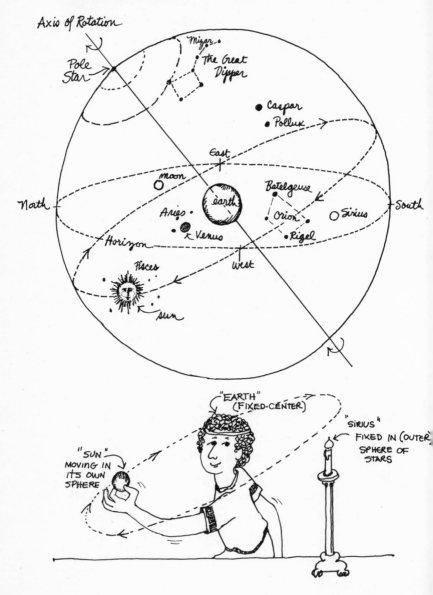

meet haughty Romans, who never spoke any language but their own, and expected everyone else—Greeks, Jews, Arabs, Ethiopians, Persians, and many others—to understand them. They all lived together in peace and harmony, working to make Alexandria greater than ever. Claudius loved to wander through the streets and listen to people talk. Having an excellent ear and a very good language sense, he soon mastered a half dozen different languages and was able to talk fluently with the people of different nationalities he met on his daily walks. He was often in the center of a group who listened, somewhat awestruck, to his fluent speech and his explanations of natural phenomena.

Claudius knew the great Alexandrian library well, but he had never run across any manuscripts of Hipparchos, who had lived some 250 years earlier and had carried out his astronomical observations in Alexandria. That pleased Claudius very much when he learned about it. He had been spending most of his time in the library reading the works of Euclid, Archimedes, and Eratosthenes. Euclid, who lived in Alexandria and did his great work on geometry there about 300 B.C., was almost worshiped by Claudius, who was to become a great geometer himself and who was then busily trying to master Euclid's thirteen books on the elements of geometry. From the writings of Archimedes, Claudius learned physics; and from the works of Eratosthenes, who was the first person to measure the size of the earth and who was head of the great library in Alexandria some fifty years after Euclid's time, Claudius learned geography.

When he began reading the works of Hipparchos, which he found among old manuscripts with his father's help, Claudius had already mastered the elements of Euclid and knew a great deal about geography. It didn't take him long to see what a great astronomer Hipparchos was and how much he had done. Hipparchos was an amazingly accurate observer. Among many other things, he described very carefully the way the sun and planets appeared to move from constellation to constellation. All that Claudius had discovered for himself was written down. In addition, there was a remarkable chart of the heavens showing the positions and giving the brightnesses of 850 different stars.

Hipparchos concluded his manuscript by describing his own theory of the solar system—the geocentric theory—with the earth fixed at the center and with the sun, moon, and planets revolving around it. This was written so well and so persuasively that it influenced Claudius very much, for he never gave up the geocentric picture of the solar system and made it the basis of the great book on astronomy he was to write later.

Claudius Ptolemy left the library that day deep in thought. He decided to devote his life to astronomy and to extend the work of Hipparchos and bring it to the attention of all who could read. But that meant doing a great deal of his own astronomical work, for there were still mysteries to be cleared up about the motions of the planets that Hipparchos had not written about.

Claudius had no trouble understanding the motions of Mars, Jupiter, and Saturn, but he was greatly puzzled by the way Mercury and Venus appeared to move. Why were these two planets never very far to the east or west of the sun? Mars, Jupiter, and Saturn moved about as though they had nothing to do with the sun; they could be found in the night sky long after the sun had set—even at midnight—as he himself had observed. But not Mercury and Venus. They behaved as though they were attached to the sun by some kind of string that could stretch to the left and to the right of the sun by only a certain amount.

If Claudius had known of the work of Aristarchus of Samos, he probably would have seen, as Aristarchus did, that there was no more mystery to the motions of Venus and Mercury than there was to the motions of Mars, Jupiter, and Saturn if all the planets, including the earth, were revolving around the sun. But Claudius was so impressed by the logic and skillful writing of Hipparchos that he accepted his geocentric theory (earth at the center of the solar system) without question. He was therefore faced with the problem of the motion of Venus and Mercury. Since Mercury is always much closer to the sun than Venus is, Mercury is very difficult to observe; it always sets shortly after the sun does or rises shortly before the sun rises. Claudius therefore decided to devote all his time to observing Venus to see if he could do what Hipparchos had been unable to do—come up with a geometrical model showing how the sun and Venus move around the earth together.

So, some four months before the trip along the Nile with his father, Claudius was faced with a great challenge—the puzzle of Venus. Night after night, as Venus moved in an eastward direction away from the sun, he observed it very carefully, but the answer didn't come to him. He felt discouraged. He lost interest in his daily activities in Alexandria and wanted to travel to some distant land; it was then that he thought of his father's trip and that it would be exciting to go.

His father was the outstanding geographer and geologist of the day. He was consulted by all who wanted to know about the mountains, the rivers, the winds, and the weather. For many years the elder Ptolemy had been studying the periodic flooding of the Nile, which was so important in the lives of the Egyptians. Every autumn, when the sun was well below the equator, and the harvesting had been completed, the Nile rose steadily because of the heavy rains near its source until it overflowed its banks and spread out over its entire delta. In doing so it deposited onto the delta lands vast amounts of rich silt carried down from the African highlands. When the Nile receded the rich, fertile soil it left behind was quickly prepared for planting; some weeks after that, the green tips of the early grains could be seen everywhere.

His father's task was to study the way in which the Nile rose as the swollen waters came down when the rains began, and he was well prepared to carry it out. During each of the five days of the journey Claudius had watched the farmers harvest the grains, hurrying as fast as they could before their lands were flooded. He was amazed at how many people—men, women, and children—worked at it. He knew that without this work Alexandrians like him and his father would starve to death, and he felt a kinship with them.

Until the fifth night of the trip Claudius hardly looked at the sky. He was so tired from traveling each day that he found himself nodding before he finished his supper, and he was fast asleep a few minutes after his last mouthful. But on the fifth night things were different. The sky was remarkably clear. Venus, at its brightest, was in the Milky Way near the constellation of Scorpius. As he looked at Venus and noted how its position had changed since he had last seen it, a sudden thought struck him that was not entirely clear but that was later to become the basis of the geocentric, or Ptolemaic, theory of the solar system. The idea, which he did not fully develop until many years later, when he wrote his famous book *The Almagest*, was that each planet moves in its own little circle about a central point, which itself moves in a much larger circle about the earth. He called these small circles *epicycles*.

To explain the difference between the motion of Venus and Mercury and the motion of the other planets, Claudius Ptolemy in time proposed the idea that the line from the earth to the sun always passes through the centers of the epicycles about which he pictured Mercury and Venus as revolving. In this way, by placing the centers of their epicycles on the line from the earth to the sun, Ptolemy kept Mercury and Venus tied to the motion of the sun, which he did not have to do with the other planets. These ideas took many years to mature, and

Ptolemy was extremely pleased when he had completed this work. He had set himself the task of explaining all the observed motions of the planets in terms of circular orbits, and he had succeeded in this. Using his epicycles he was able to account for all the observed planetary motions, and he felt that the time had come to write a book about it. He began writing one of the famous books in the history of thought and science, the *Great System of Astronomy*. This was later translated into Arabic and shortened to *The Almagest*, and that is what people have called it ever since.

When he had finished this book, which took many years to write because it consisted of thirteen separate books and covered all of known astronomy, geography, mathematics, and physics, he had explained everything. He was happiest, however, about his idea about epicycles. He stated: "Whosoever thinks my construction too artificial should remember that uniform motion in a circle corresponds to divine nature. To reduce all apparent irregularities to such motion may well be called a feat. Thereby the ultimate goal of philosophy and science is attained."

We know today that Ptolemy's epicycles and his geocentric theory are wrong, but we must admire his great skill as a scholar, a mathematician, and a writer. He wrote so skillfully and explained things so logically that *The Almagest* became a kind of bible of science. Until the fifteenth century it was the most accurate and, in fact, the only description of the heavens that took into account all the astronomical observations of that period. Claudius

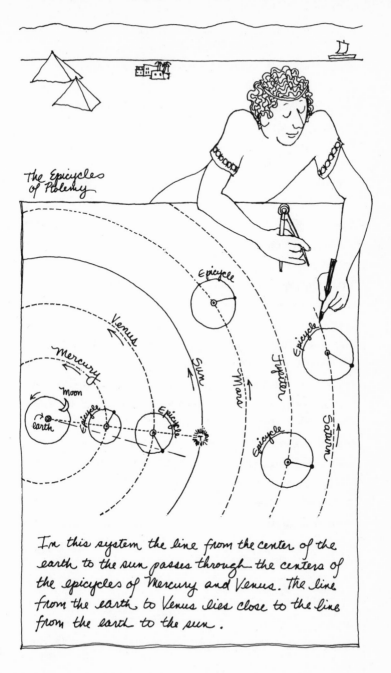

The Epicycles
of Ptolemy

Epicycle

Venus

Mercury

Moon

earth

Epicycle

Epicycle

Sun

Mars

Jupiter

Epicycle

Epicycle

Saturn

Epicycle

In this system the line from the center of the
earth to the sun passes through the centers of
the epicycles of Mercury and Venus. The line
from the earth to Venus lies close to the line
from the earth to the sun.

Ptolemy lived out his life in Alexandria as a greatly revered astronomer, scholar, and writer, and for fifteen hundred years after his death most people accepted his geocentric theory of the solar system as correct.

"So that's why Aristarchus's heliocentric theory of the solar system took so long to catch on," thought Michael as he finished reading the last page of the Ptolemy story. "It was Ptolemy, with his very clever book, and his very clear explanation of the geocentric theory, and his epicycles, who kept people from thinking about any other theory until Copernicus came along," Michael said to himself. Many questions popped into his mind as he thought of how great an influence *The Almagest* had had on man's thinking. Suppose Ptolemy had studied the works of Aristarchus as thoroughly as he had studied Hipparchus, and had accepted his heliocentric theory and written about it in *The Almagest*. Wouldn't mankind and civilization be much further advanced than they are now? He soon realized how fruitless such thoughts were.

Darkness had begun to settle over the room, and Michael saw that it was almost suppertime. There was no time that night to go on to the third story. He left the manuscript on his father's desk open to the first page of that story, planning to come back to it the next day.

4=NICOLAS COPERNICUS AND THE BOOK OF THE REVOLUTIONS

It had been incredibly cold that winter, so cold that the frozen ground had cracked in spots, and the Vistula River was frozen to a depth of five feet. Nobody could remember days as cold as these. Some people said the world was coming to an end, that there would be no more springs or summers and everyone would either freeze or starve to death. The peasants had lost some of their livestock from freezing, and they were complaining that there was not enough grain to feed their animals or enough fuel to warm them. From his bedroom window, young Nicolas could see the bonfires they lighted at darkness and kept going all night near their animal shelters. He had heard that the wise men of Torun were saying that God was punishing people for straying from the true Catholic faith and following the teachings of heretics and false prophets. He was frightened by such talk. Whenever he heard it he would quickly go over the catechism in his mind, to reassure himself that he was still a good Catholic and would somehow or other escape the dreadful fate that the heretics would suffer.

But there was something about this kind of punishment that did not agree with Nicolas's idea of a just and reasonable God. Why punish the many good and kind people for the sins of a few? The more Nicolas thought about it, the more convinced he was that God would not interfere with the laws of nature and the orderly advance of the seasons just to punish a few heretics. Spring, summer, and fall with its rich harvest would come again, and the world would go on in its orderly way obeying the laws of nature and God.

Comforted as he was by these simple ideas, Nicolas still had to confess to himself that this particular day—February 19 and his birthday—was by far the coldest yet. The cold had even crept into the elegant room in his uncle's house in which he was now sitting, deep in thought, warming himself at the large fireplace and staring intently at the leaping flames. Even as he wondered at the beautiful patterns wrought by the flames and felt their warmth, he could hear the tread of boots every now and then across the snow-packed street on which the large house stood. The snow was so hard and cold that the sounds of the footsteps were almost like metal striking glass, and they chilled him.

Occasionally Nicolas walked across the room to look through one of the clear panes of the large stained-glass window of which Uncle Lucas was so proud. It was, indeed, a very beautiful window, arranged in such a way that the rays of the late afternoon sun, passing through the colored panes of glass, filled the room with a wondrous light which his uncle called the "glory of God." It had a strange effect on all the objects in the room, and it softened the glowering features of Lucas Watzelrode in his large portrait that hung above the fireplace. At such times, as at this very moment, Nicolas could see his mother's face in the portrait, behind the features of Uncle Lucas, and he wondered how two people who looked so much alike could be so different.

The sun was setting quickly as Nicolas watched the busy scene on the river below. Cold as it was, people were skating on the Vistula, his older brother Andreas, whom he adored, among them. Many fires had been built, not only along the shore of the river, but also on the ice itself, and almost as many skaters were huddled about the fires as were skating. He tried to pick out his brother's red skating hat and red scarf from among the skaters, but he couldn't among the shadows cast by the sun.

It had been a busy day in the Watzelrode household, for two events were being celebrated that day: Nicolas's sixteenth birthday and the appointment of Uncle Lucas as the new bishop of Ermland, a province that lay some miles to the northeast, with its cathedral in Frauenburg, a city on the Baltic Sea. In the early afternoon the long table in the luxurious dining room had been splendidly set with liquor, wines, and foods of all kinds, and more than twenty people had sat around it. Uncle Lucas, at its head, ate and drank enormously. As usual, Lucas dominated and intimidated everyone with his loud voice and rude talk. Nicolas was not sure whether he liked or disliked his uncle, who had assumed responsibility for Nicolas's education when his father died, but he knew that he feared him somewhat and rarely spoke out or expressed his opinion in front of him for fear of being reprimanded and bullied, as his mother often was when she spoke to her brother. Nicolas, watching his mother cringe before the loud voice, as though being whipped, hated his uncle at such moments. But that feeling never lasted very long, for Lucas Watzelrode had done much for Nicolas, his mother, his brother, and his two younger sisters. Nicolas was grateful to him for that.

In spite of what Uncle Lucas said and did, the party was a success. Everyone—all the important citizens of Torun were there—enjoyed himself. Nicolas was upset at one point when his uncle, after offering a toast to himself as the new bishop, offered another to Nicolas on his birthday and announced that Nicolas was to go to the University of Cracow soon to study medicine and law. He didn't stop there. He stated that Nicolas was also to become a canon of Frauenburg Cathedral when the old canon died. Nicolas was disturbed at that because he had planned an entirely different life for himself which did not include law, medicine, or religious studies. He was happiest when he was thinking about the heavens and the mysteries presented by the motions of the heavenly bodies. To devote his life to the task of explaining those mysteries was his greatest hope; but if his uncle wanted him to study medicine or law and to become a canon of the church, he would do so.

His brother, Andreas, was not as meek as Nicolas. He often spoke up to Uncle Lucas, which Nicolas greatly, and secretly, admired. Nobody knew where and how Andreas spent his time when he was not in the house. Today, after the party, Andreas had invited Nicolas to skate with him, but Nicolas was too timid to go. He did not skate well and hated the cold, which he could almost taste as he watched the skaters. Moreover, he felt uncomfortable in the presence of Andreas's rough companions.

The year was 1489, some thirteen hundred and fifty years after Ptolemy had written *The Almagest*, which Nicolas had read from cover to cover and knew almost by heart. Everything in the book excited him, but nothing more than Ptolemy's geocentric theory of the solar system and its many epicycles. Nicolas admired Ptolemy's mathematical skill and how cleverly he had introduced one epicycle after another to explain the observed motions of the planets. He particularly admired the way Ptolemy kept Venus and Mercury close to the sun by keeping the centers of their epicycles on the line from the earth to the sun. But in spite of his admiration for Ptolemy, he felt something was wrong with the whole thing. There were just too many epicycles in the Ptolemaic theory. The number of epicycles since the time of Ptolemy had grown like weeds, until there were now about one hundred different epicycles. All were needed to explain the present observations; and still others would have to be introduced as more accurate observations of the planets were made.

It was clear to Nicolas that any observed motion of a planet could be explained if one introduced enough epicycles. As he saw it, the trouble with Ptolemy's picture was that it was just too complicated. There had to be a much simpler way to explain the whole thing, and Nicolas felt he was destined to discover that way. He already saw that taking the earth out of the center of the solar system, where Ptolemy had fixed it, and placing the sun there instead, would greatly simplify things; but he had no proof for such a revolutionary idea and was uncertain as to how to prove such a thing. He didn't know enough astronomy at that young stage of his life to construct a new theory of the solar system, but he had decided to devote his life to it. He was confident he would succeed in time.

Such were the thoughts that raced through Nicolas's mind that cold afternoon of his sixteenth birthday. As he walked back to the fireplace, he suddenly recalled how he was first attracted to astronomy. It had something to do with Venus. During the summer of six years ago, a few months before his father died, the family had gone on a picnic. The forested hills to the south of Torun were beautiful and fragrant in late June and early July with the mountain laurel, the rhododendron, and the wild phlox in full bloom. Those wild flowers, together with the sweet fern and the ripening blueberries, huckleberries, and juneberries, cast such a magic spell over the forest that the ten-year-old Nicolas thought it was bewitched that summer. He loved to wander off by himself on clear days, following the Vistula southward to his own magic spots in the wooded hills, but he never went far because of his fears of getting lost and of wild animals. The peasants told many stories of people being devoured by wolves, and Nicolas believed every word even though Andreas told him over and over again that they were just fairy tales and that wolves rarely came into woods near a city during the summer months.

His favorite spot was a moss-covered area on the side of a hill facing the town, which was hidden from sight. The spot itself was surrounded by pines, maples, oak and birch trees; and though he could not see the river, he could hear a nearby brook that fed into it. Nicolas loved to lie here marveling at the intricate forms of the occasional clouds in the sky and listening to the wind in the trees and the plaintive song of the wood thrush. The magic of the woods aroused in him such a sense of wonder that he felt as though his mind would burst with it. There was so much to think about, so much to understand. How would he ever answer all the questions that rose in his mind like bubbles in boiling water? Though many ideas and questions came and went through his mind as he lay on the moss, one always remained. How high was the sky and how far did it extend?

Those were very happy days for Nicolas. His father was alive then, and he remembered how joyfully the whole family looked forward to their outings during the summer months. The beginning of summer, June 21, was always celebrated by a picnic; it was the longest day of the year, and the picnic and daylight seemed to last forever.

On that particular June 21, almost six years ago, Nicolas had fallen asleep gazing at the sky, his head in his mother's lap. The swaying trees and her gentle lullaby, no louder than the rustle of the leaves, had hypnotized him. When he awoke, it was getting dark. Venus and the brightest stars were visible in the western sky. Although he had often seen Venus before, he was startled by its brilliance at that moment. All he knew about the planet was what his father had told him, and that was not very much—no more than Aristarchus or Ptolemy knew—that it was a heavenly body that revolved around the earth and shifted from one side to the other of the sun periodically. Knowledge about Venus had advanced very little in the thousands of years since the ancient Greeks. But as Nicolas looked at it, he had a premonition that in some manner, the rest of his life would be closely associated with Venus and the other planets.

Turning his gaze from the sky, he suddenly sensed that he was alone and was frightened until he heard his mother's voice telling Andreas and his sisters to gather the picnic things because it was time to go home. As they walked toward Torun in the half darkness, Nicolas kept thinking of Venus and wondering about its mysterious movements across the sky. His father had told him that Venus and Mercury were the only planets whose movements were tied to the movement of the sun, and that when Nicolas was older and had learned enough to read the works of Ptolemy, he would find a very clever explanation for this behavior of Venus and Mercury in Ptolemy's *Almagest.*

Nicolas knew that arrangements were being made for him to study with a special tutor at the end of the summer, but the sudden death of his father, Niklas Koppernigk, changed everything. Uncle Lucas Watzelrode entered his life and took control of the family.

The six years had passed quickly. Nicolas, who had changed the spelling of his name from Koppernigk to the simpler Latin form Copernicus, had studied languages, mathematics, geography, and astronomy with a tutor hired by his uncle. The young Copernicus gave more and more time to his books and spent long hours thinking about what he read. His great passion was still astronomy, and most of his thinking was devoted to it; but he rarely made any astronomical observations or measurements. He knew that his strength lay, not in looking at the heavenly bodies, but in thinking about them and trying to construct a geometrical model to explain their motions.

As the sun set and the room in his uncle's house grew dark, Nicolas knew that one phase of his life would soon be coming to an end, and another would begin. He had mastered all that the Torun school and his tutors could teach him, and it was only a matter of time before he would be leaving Torun to attend the University of Cracow. The idea of going to Cracow excited Nicolas. His parents had come from there, and Uncle Lucas had often spoken of the magnificence of the city and the excellence of its university, which attracted students from all over Europe. The University of Cracow was especially famous for its school of mathematics and astronomy, and that is what attracted Nicolas most. He hoped that his uncle would permit him to begin studying astronomy even though he would have to study law and medicine in time.

On his eighteenth birthday, in the year 1491, Nicolas Copernicus, sad at having to leave his family and the woods of Torun, where so many ideas had come to him, enrolled at the University at Cracow with his uncle's permission and blessings. He came to study astronomy with the famous Polish astronomer, Albert of Brudzew, whose book on the Ptolemaic theory of the solar system was the standard text for students throughout Europe at that time. He came hoping that all his questions about the planets would be answered, but they were not. The four years of intense reading and thinking that he did while at Cracow strengthened his belief that Ptolemy was wrong, but how to replace the system of Ptolemy with his own system eluded him. He read everything he could lay his hands on which might help him in his great project, from the writings of the ancient Greeks to the works of Brudzew; but the more he read, the more convinced he was that he had little to learn from Ptolemy and from others who thought as he did.

Though he found little to support his idea of a heliocentric (sun at center) solar system, two things encouraged Nicolas to go on. One was the great difference of opinion about the motion of the earth he found among various philosophers, and the other was that others before him believed that the earth moves. The work of Aristarchus had been forgotten, but the idea that the earth moves was proposed, without any explanation, every now and then by certain scholars such as Cicero and Plutarch. Although encouraged by such opinions, Nicolas was tortured by doubts. He spent sleepless nights worrying about being ridiculed if he were bold enough to propose his own heliocentric theory. He needed proof, but where was he to find such proof? Very few observations of the planets had been made since the time of Ptolemy and hardly any accurate measurements of their motions. He began to realize that he might never be able to prove his theory and that the best he could hope for would be to show that it was a simpler and more plausible theory than Ptolemy's.

Except for his teacher, Albert of Brudzew, who was devoted to the Ptolemaic theory and hence not sympathetic to his ideas, Nicolas had met no one at Cracow with whom he could discuss his theory. His brother, Andreas, who was also at Cracow at that time, had no interest in astronomy and understood little of what Nicolas tried to tell him. And so, after four years at Cracow, at the age of twenty-two, Nicolas was not unhappy to return to Torun at his uncle's bidding. He knew why Lucas Watzelrode, who was now bishop of Ermland, wanted him in Torun. It was to appoint him a canon of Frauenburg Cathedral when one of the old canons died. But things didn't turn out quite that way immediately, and Nicolas had to wait two more years to be appointed. By that time he was content to earn his livelihood as a church official; his uncle had told him that there would be little real work for him to do as a canon, and he could spend as much time as he pleased studying the planets.

The beautiful summer of 1496 was coming to an end in Torun, and Nicolas had just returned from one of his daily afternoon walks into the southern hills. He was in the same room in which his sixteenth birthday had been celebrated when his uncle entered. He was in a happier mood than usual, a warm, somewhat tender look on his face. He greeted his nephew and announced that Nicolas had just been appointed a canon of Frauenburg. That wasn't all. The duties at Frauenburg were so light, his uncle went on, that Nicolas need not go there immediately. He could continue his studies, but this time he was to go to the great Italian universities of Bologna and Padua to study law and medicine, as he had promised, as well as astronomy. Nicolas greeted these announcements with mixed feelings. He wanted to please his uncle and so he was prepared to go to Italy, but the idea of studying law and medicine and taking time away from his contemplation of the solar system disturbed him.

Nevertheless, he spent the next ten years of his life in Bologna, Padua, and Rome. When he returned to Poland in 1506 to take up his duties as canon at Frauenburg, at the age of thirty-three, he had obtained degrees in law and medicine. A good deal more had also happened to him. In the year 1500, at the age of twenty-seven, he had been invited to lecture on mathematics and astronomy before "a throng of great men and experts in the field," which shows that he had become known to scholars as a brilliant astronomer even while mastering law and medicine. That event was very important to him, for it greatly increased his self-confidence as an astronomer and forced him to formulate and state his ideas exactly and clearly.

From that time onward, Nicolas Copernicus knew what he had to do, and how he was to construct his heliocentric theory of the solar system, a theory that was to revolutionize man's thinking about the universe. The light religious duties he had as a canon, and the occasional practice of medicine, left him with all the time he needed to work out his theory.

From all he had read and observed, he saw that the stars formed a system of very distant bodies quite apart from the sun, moon, and planets. He reasoned, from the way the stars looked, that they must be at much greater distances from the earth than the planets. Since, as far as he knew, the constellations had never been observed to change their shapes or their relative positions, either the stars were rigidly held together in some way or they *were* moving about, but were so far away that the human eye could not detect any changes in their relative positions even in many lifetimes. Although Copernicus had no proof, he preferred to believe that the stars were at enormous distances from the earth.

"How simple it all is," he thought to himself. "The stars are very far away and rise and set every day not because the sky is turning around the earth, but because the earth itself rotates once a day. If the stars, at such vast distances, revolved around the earth once a day, they would have to travel at such enormous speeds that nothing could hold them in place. The whole stellar universe would fly apart." He was happy with this simple explanation of the rising and setting of the stars, and saw that the daily rising and setting of the sun, moon, and planets was explained at the same time. It made much more sense to Copernicus to have one body—the earth—spin than to have everything else in the universe spin around a fixed earth.

Having come to the conclusion that the earth is spinning, he could find no logical objection to having it move about as well. That would explain everything. "If the earth were moving eastward around a fixed sun," he reasoned, "the sun would not appear to be fixed in the sky but instead would appear to move eastward from constellation to constellation tracing out the circle in the sky which is known as the ecliptic." And so he arrived at the same conclusion as Aristarchus had.

"So far, so good," he thought, "but what about the planets? They appear to move not only to the east, from constellation to constellation, as the sun does, but they also cut back and move to the west from time to time, describing loops in the sky. Can I explain that by having the earth revolve around the sun? Yes, if at the same time I have each planet move in its own orbit around the sun."

He was jubilant at this idea. He saw at once that such an arrangement would get rid of the problem presented by the apparent motions of Venus and Mercury, which tied them to the sun in a curious way that did not apply to the other three planets. Ptolemy had explained the

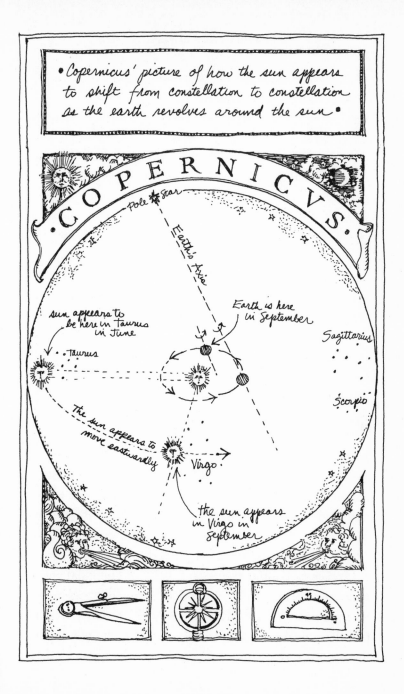

• Copernicus' picture of how the sun appears to shift from constellation to constellation as the earth revolves around the sun •

·COPERNICVS·

Pole Star

Earth's Axis

sun appears to be here in Taurus in June

Earth is here in September

Sagittarius

·Taurus

Scorpio

The sun appears to move eastwardly

Virgo

the sun appears in Virgo in September

observed motions of all the known planets with his famous epicycles, but Copernicus did not like Ptolemy's epicycles because Venus and Mercury had to be treated in a special way and given special epicycles, whose centers were always on the line from the earth to the sun. Such an arrangement was not necessary for Mars, Jupiter, or Saturn. This special treatment of the two inner planets in Ptolemy's scheme disturbed Copernicus.

Nicolas was a perfectionist. He felt that there must be a flaw in any system that did not apply the same principles to all the planets. In Copernicus's system this nonuniformity was eliminated. By having all the planets, including the earth, revolve around the sun, Copernicus had unified the system. All the planets had the same kind of motion now—they all moved around the sun in the same direction and in the same kind of orbits. The only difference between the motions of Venus and Mercury and those of the other three planets was in the sizes of their orbits around the sun. Copernicus saw that if the orbits of Venus and Mercury around the sun were smaller than the earth's orbit, these two planets would always appear to swing from one side of the sun to the other. And with Venus moving in a larger orbit than Mercury, it would have a larger swing on either side of the sun than Mercury; as, indeed, it does have. The orbits of Mars, Jupiter, and Saturn, on the other hand, would have to be larger than the earth's orbit because the motions of these three planets do not appear to be related to the sun's apparent motion.

Nicolas was very happy with this solution. "We must keep in mind," he reasoned, "that the way a planet appears to move, as we watch it from the earth, is a combination of the planet's true motion around the sun and the earth's motion around the sun. We can obtain the true motion of the planet only if we take into account the earth's motion."

With that simple idea Copernicus swept away thirteen hundred years of wrong thinking. But his need for perfection led him into error. To him, perfection meant constant speed in a circular orbit, and so he assigned circular orbits to the earth and the other planets. Copernicus was thus forced to use some epicycles in his theory because in fact orbits are not circles. By combining enough epicycles, each of which is a circle, Copernicus obtained good agreement between his heliocentric theory and with the observations. And he needed fewer than half the epicycles Ptolemy had introduced.

Only after Nicolas had returned to Poland did he begin to write down his ideas about the solar system, and in 1530 he completed the manuscript that was not to be published until thirteen years later. *The Book of Revolutions of the Heavenly Spheres* is perhaps the most important book in the history of ideas, but Nicolas was very reluctant to publish it.

After the sudden death of his uncle in 1512, Copernicus had gone to Frauenburg to carry on his duties as canon and to complete his manuscript. He lived peacefully there and lectured on his theory to all who would listen. He even allowed some people to read his manuscript and to copy parts of it. These copies were passed from hand to hand so that Nicolas's fame as an astronomer grew throughout Europe, but he steadfastly refused to publish his work. Copernicus was a lonely man with few friends. He loved solitude above all else and was fearful that the calm quality of his life would be disturbed if too many people learned about his theory. Moreover, he was afraid he might be ridiculed for his strange ideas—"hissed off the stage," as he put it, "and in fear of the scorn which my new and absurd opinion would bring upon me." Finally, after much persuasion by his friends and students, he allowed his book to be published. The first printed copy reached him on his deathbed thirteen years after he had finished writing it. He died before he saw it.

This book, with all its errors and wrong ideas about circular orbits for the planets, opened the door to modern astronomy. The unity in the motions of the planets that Copernicus sought and knew that he had found is stated in the following short passage taken from his book: "that what appears to be a motion of the sun is in truth a motion of the earth; but that the size of the universe is so great, that the distance of the earth from the sun though appreciable . . . is as nothing when compared to that of the sphere of the fixed stars. And I hold it easier to concede this than let the mind be distracted by an almost endless multitude of circles (epicycles) which those are obliged to do who detain the earth in the center of the world. The wisdom of nature is such that it produces

The earth's orbit according to Copernicus

earth
epicycle
P
C
sun
epicycle

In the Copernican system the sun is not at the center of the earth's circle. The center of the earth's circle is a point C which revolves in an epicycle around a point P which revolves in another epicycle around the sun. Thus Copernicus required 2 epicycles to describe the earth's motion.

nothing superfluous or useless but often produces many effects from one cause."

When Michael finished reading the story of Nicolas Copernicus, he felt disappointed and let down—almost as though Copernicus, one of his heroes, had betrayed him. He had always thought of Copernicus as a fearless thinker, who defied authority and boldly proclaimed his revolutionary ideas. But that wasn't so at all. He was really quite timid and cautious.

"They had to beg him to write his book, and then he apologized for what he wrote before he even wrote it, and he didn't do so much anyway. It was all guesswork," thought Michael. He searched his mind for something that might restore Copernicus to his former glory, but he could find nothing. As he left the library to get ready for dinner, Michael wondered sadly which of his other heroes would fall from their pedestals. If Copernicus could fall, who was safe? Maybe he was being unfair to Copernicus after all, maybe there was more to what Copernicus had done than what Michael's father had written.

And this was true. Michael was to see that Copernicus had done much more than propose a theory he could not prove. He had written down in fairly precise and very persuasive language a theory that appealed to other great thinkers who followed him. Thus he started a revolution in human thinking.

5~ AT THE
DINNER TABLE

His mother, father, and sister were already seated at the table when Michael entered the dining room. They were waiting for him before starting their dinner. He felt sorry for causing the delay, but no one at the table showed any annoyance. They were talking gaily and greeted Michael as pleasantly as ever. It had always been this way, it seemed to Michael, and he thought how wonderful it would be if it never changed. The bowl of fresh flowers at the center of the table with a lighted candle on either side; the white tablecloth and napkins; the dishes with delicate pink flowers along their rims; the sparkling silverware, neatly arranged on both sides of each dinner plate; the fragrance of warm, freshly buttered rolls; above all, the chatter and laughter of the three people he loved most.

The dinner hour was the happiest time of day for Michael, and often the most exciting because of the many things that were discussed. His father or mother would generally start some topic going and in a few minutes they were all at it, saying things that ranged from clever to most outlandish. In the midst of the most serious discussion his father had a way of saying clearly ridiculous things that brought peals of laughter from them all—even from his mother who, at the same time, showed her annoyance at the interruption. Jessica, Michael's sister, was two years younger than he and wasn't always sure she was supposed to laugh. She would quickly turn to her father for a slight wink that told her he was spoofing. There was something in the relationship between Jessica and her father that Michael at times envied—like a wondrous secret that could never be told or understood. Jessica rarely discussed science with her father, but there were times when she asked him question after question about astronomy, and he answered each one as simply as possible while she sat listening to him wide-eyed and intent.

Throughout dinner, Michael had done very little talking as the conversation went from Jessica's coming birthday party to a discussion of his father's trip to an international astronomy conference in Europe. Michael was still bothered about Copernicus, but he didn't feel like breaking into the general conversation with a direct question. His chance to introduce his question came just before dessert when his father announced that he had arranged for his entire family to meet him in Greece after the conference. They were to spend the first two weeks of their summer vacation traveling through the Greek islands and then go on to Poland for another scientific conference. When his father announced this, Michael asked whether they would stop at Samos.

"Why Samos?" his mother asked. "What is so special about it, Michael?"

"It is one of the Greek islands that dad has written a story about, mother."

"A story? A true story or fiction about Samos? I didn't know your father wrote fiction. Scientists are not supposed to write fiction. But I suppose some scientists do write fiction without knowing it," she said teasingly.

Her husband smiled at this while Michael frowned and Jessica looked puzzled.

"It's a true story, mother, although I think some of it is fiction," Michael answered.

"How can something be a true story and fiction at the same time?" said Jessica.

"Well, it's a story about a Greek astronomer named Aristarchus when he was a boy a long time ago," said Michael. "And it could have been true, but I don't know whether things really happened the way dad described them."

"You are right, Michael," said his father. "Very little is known about the life of Aristarchus, but we do know that he believed that the sun is fixed at the center of the solar system and that the planets, including the earth, revolve around it. Today Aristarchus is known as the Greek Copernicus."

"But, dad, your story is about Aristarchus when he was my age. How do you know what kind of boy he was?" asked Michael.

"I don't, nor does anyone," answered his father, "so I had to guess at it. But we do know what kind of man Aristarchus was, and from that we can figure out what kind of boy he might have been. The same thing is true of Ptolemy, Copernicus, and the others you will read about in those stories I wrote."

"I want to read them, too," cried Jessica.

"Of course you may read them, Jessica," her father replied. "There may be parts you won't understand completely, but I think you'll find the stories interesting."

"What I don't see," said Michael, "is how Aristarchus, Ptolemy, and Copernicus could have done what dad claims they did when they were my age."

His father looked thoughtfully at Michael for a moment and said, "These were not ordinary bright boys. They were boys who were to grow up to become some of the greatest scientists of all time. As they were very unusual men, so they were very unusual boys. We have many examples in modern times of incredibly brilliant young people who did remarkable things when they were even younger than you—more remarkable than what Aristarchus and Ptolemy did. The great German mathematician Karl Friedrich Gauss, for instance, discovered a mathematical theorem when he was six or seven years old. The remarkable Hindu mathematician Ramanujan mastered very complicated mathematics before he was thirteen. By the time he was twenty he had proved complex theorems that had stumped the best mathematicians in Europe. Unfortunately, he died quite young—when he was only thirty-three. Einstein began to think about the nature of light when he was sixteen, and he saw even then that there is something remarkable about the speed of light."

"I know what it is," said Jessica. "Nothing can travel as fast as light."

"That was almost it, Jessica," her father continued. "Einstein almost came up with that idea. But when Einstein at sixteen thought about the speed of light, very little was known about light. The great Italian physicist Enrico Fermi was doing advanced physics when he was fourteen, as was Lorentz, the Dutch physicist."

"Something bothers me about Copernicus," said Michael. "I really don't think his work was so great. He had no proof for his theory. It was all guesswork, and he still had to use epicycles."

"Don't be too hasty, Michael," his father replied. "It is true that Copernicus had no proof that the earth spins daily and revolves around the sun every year. To prove that the earth revolves around the sun one has to make very careful and accurate observations of the stars, with a good telescope and such observations weren't made until hundreds of years after Copernicus died. Copernicus had no telescope and he was not really an observer. He was a dreamer and a thinker who felt that the motion of all the planets, including the earth, should be governed by the same laws. In that way he was like Aristarchus, who had no proof for his heliocentric theory, but who knew that it must be right because it replaced many unrelated motions by a single kind of motion for the earth and the planets. Both men were seeking the underlying unity in nature.

"Copernicus disliked the Ptolemaic theory because it meant having one set of laws for Mercury and Venus, another set for the sun and the moon, another set for the earth alone, and a fourth set for Mars, Jupiter, and Saturn. True, Copernicus still had to use epicycles in his theory of the solar system because he used circular orbits for the planets, but that doesn't diminish his work at all. Remember that for thousands of years people had believed the earth was fixed. It took a lot of courage to put the sun at the center of the solar system and have the earth and the other planets revolve around it. That was the great thing that Copernicus did—it unified everything and revolutionized man's thinking. That one idea, which Copernicus insisted on and which he never gave up, is why he was so great a man."

Michael would have liked to carry on the discussion, but dinner was over. His mother had already risen from her chair to start clearing the table, and that was generally a signal for him and Jessica to help.

When Michael returned to his father's library after school the next day, he felt a good deal better about Copernicus. He was even ready to restore him to his former place among his heroes. But he was still disappointed that at the time of Copernicus so few accurate observations had been made. Astronomy at that time was still guesswork. It was not an exact science. It was with this feeling that Michael sat down to read the next episode in his father's narration.

6-TYCHO
BRAHE AND THE
CITY IN THE SKY

The proud, arrogant nobleman at the head of the vast table heaped with food and drink looked with contempt at the people seated around it gorging themselves as fast as they could.

"All they can think of," he said to himself, "are horses, dogs, and luxury. A useless bunch, who come to my island to carouse and stuff themselves at my expense. They court me for my fame and my knowledge and not because they care one iota about me. The peasants and vassals who serve me are more valuable than are these idlers and buffoons."

It mattered not that princes, dukes, and even kings might be among the people seated at his table. They counted for little in his eyes, and yet he loved to entertain them on a grand scale and to show off the magnificence of his court, his observatory, and his island. Not even the most powerful rulers could put on the kind of show that he could, or overwhelm their guests with celestial and occult mysteries as he did. He had the key that could open the door to the universe, and they had come to him to pass through the door.

He smiled as he thought of their awe-struck faces and the wonder in their eyes when they first entered his observatory and saw the huge celestial globes, the armillaries, the giant quadrants, and the other astronomical instruments under the mighty dome of the observatory. All these instruments, among which the quadrant was the most important, were naked-eye devices. His quadrant consisted of the arc of a circle, about five times the height of a man, with a crossbar along which he could sight any celestial object and measure its position with amazing accuracy. "My miracle instruments," he called them as he caressed them fondly.

He had designed each one of them according to the most precise geometrical laws and had supervised their construction with the greatest care. He insisted that they be the most accurate instruments ever made, and when they were finished, they were more precious to him than anything or anyone else. These were machines the like of which the world had never seen. They were worthy of him—an observer the like of which the world had never seen nor would ever see again. It pleased him to think that they were housed in the most splendid observatory ever built and which he had designed. It was a monstrous four-story structure, built like a fortress, with every known astronomical device in it. In the basement there were special cells in which he imprisoned workers or peasants who displeased him, for he insisted on absolute obedience. "Without obedience and precise adherence to rules, nothing can be accomplished," he would often say. Nature was precise, and man had to be precise if he were to be true to nature.

He cared not that people disliked him or feared him. He wanted only one thing in life—to make the most accurate and precise astronomical measurements and observations ever made. Everybody in his establishment had to work toward that end.

To be precise in everything astronomical was a passion with this remarkable man who was born Tycho Brahe, but who was called Tyge by those close to him. He was famous throughout Europe for his skill as an observer— people knew that his naked-eye observations of the stars and the planets were ten times more accurate than any that had been made in the past. He knew that people knew this, and it gave him a sense of power, for everyone considered him a great astrologer as well; people came from all over to have their horoscopes cast.

"They are foolish and stupid," he thought. "I believe little of this nonsense. But let them come if they want to. It amuses me to cast horoscopes and to astound people with my predictions. Let them have respect for me and my astronomical skill one way or another. If it's through astrology, fine. The more they respect and honor me, whether for astrology or astronomy, the easier it will be for me to get the money I need for my observatory. That's all that matters."

Tycho drank and ate along with the others at his table

as the feast went on. From time to time he took some ointment from a small, delicate snuffbox to rub along the tip of his nose as though to relieve a pain or an itch. Nobody dared look too closely at Tyge's nose, for part of it was not really his. A careful inspection would have shown that the tip of his nose was not flesh at all. It was an alloy of silver and gold that had been pasted on with putty. The fine thin line where his real nose ended and the fake piece was attached could be faintly seen.

Tycho's vanity had caused him to lose the end of his nose in a duel when he was still a university student. He could not tolerate having anyone outdo him in anything, whether it was eating, drinking, arguing, or mathematics. At the university, he was explaining an obscure mathematical point to some classmates one evening when a stranger questioned his logic and his mathematical ability. Enraged at the interruption, Tycho challenged him to a duel which they fought on the spot, and mostly in the dark. Before the duel was over, Tycho had lost the tip of his nose and some of his pride. He brooded for a while about it and worried about his appearance until he fashioned the silver-gold tip which he attached to his nose every day.

The noise in the large dining room was almost deafening as the musicians at one end of the room competed with the shouting, laughing guests, and with the barking dogs who scrambled for bits of food that fell from the table. It all amused Tycho. From time to time, he threw bits of food to his jester, Jepp, a dwarf of whom he was very fond. Jepp always sat on a stool at Tycho's right hand and kept Tycho amused by a stream of clever and witty remarks. People feared Jepp because they thought he could read the future and could cast spells, so they rarely crossed him. Being friendly with Jepp was one way of staying on the good side of Tycho.

As the evening wore on and the noise subsided, the guests, one by one, dropped off to sleep. Tycho, too, grew drowsy and dreamed of the many things he had done, and all that remained to be done. He was now fifty years old; and the sixteenth century had only four more years to go. What a glorious century it had been! The century of the greatest literature, the greatest works of art, the greatest developments of religion, the greatest astronomy, and the greatest astronomer. It was only proper that his work crowned it all. But he knew an era was coming to an end, and he wondered what lay ahead. He had a feeling that his whole life was to change, that things would never again be as they had been; and he feared and yet welcomed the change that was to come.

For weeks now he had been bored with everything, even with his astronomy. He had made thousands of observations and countless measurements, but what did it all mean? What did it all amount to? He was filled with doubts that took the pleasure from his work. To go on making more and more measurements and observations just for their own sake made no sense. If his life's work was to be meaningful, he had to use all those measurements and observations to construct a correct theory of the motions of the planets and the sun. But he didn't know how to do it.

He could make very precise observations of the positions of the planets and the sun as they moved among the stars, but to construct or deduce correct orbits from his own observations was beyond him. He didn't have the mathematical skill or the creativity to do it. He cursed himself for not having studied more mathematics when he was young. He had to get some brilliant, ambitious young mathematician to help him. Someone like that crazy German fellow. What was his name? A name that began with *K;* an unusual name—Kepler. Johannes Kepler. That was it. A very strange fellow, indeed, but extremely brilliant. Kepler had written a few letters to him in which Kepler explained some of his ideas. They sounded crazy, but they were developed with such mathematical mastery that Tyge was greatly impressed. How could he get Kepler to work with him?

A loud noise disturbed Tycho's reveries. He looked up to see two of his guests at the farther end of the table in a violent hand-to-hand fight. He cursed them under his breath as he lurched from his chair and walked unsteadily toward them. Jepp, having run ahead, was dancing wildly around the struggling pair and chanting some kind of doggerel when Tycho got there. Taking each one by the collar, and with as little effort as though he were handling children, Tycho yanked the two fighting guests apart and flung them to the floor. For a moment they were stunned, but they soon recovered their senses. When they saw the glowering face above them, they got to their feet quietly and shambled off to their quarters. Tycho walked back to

As the earth revolves around the sun a nearby star appears to shift back and forth every six months.

Eye of observer in June

Eye of observer in December

Earth in December

Earth in June

Star

Background Stars

his chair, arranged his body exactly as it was before, and went back to his thoughts.

Where had he left off? He remembered now. He was thinking of that German genius Kepler. He must get hold of Kepler and persuade him to work on the Tychonic system of the world: a system Tycho had invented but could not prove was correct. It was obvious to him that it combined the best features of the Ptolemaic system and the Copernican system. It was beautiful, thought Tycho, and no one could really object to it.

"Copernicus was right in one respect," he said to himself. "The planets do revolve around the sun. But Copernicus was wrong in thinking that the earth moves— that the earth revolves around the sun. No! The earth must be fixed. If it were revolving around the sun, it would carry us first to one side of the sun and then to the other and the stars would then appear to shift back and forth every six months just the way my finger does when I hold it up and look at it first with one eye and then with the other. If my two eyes were separated by the distance between the two positions of the earth when it is on either side of the sun, and I measured the position of a star as viewed first with one eye on one side of the sun and then with the other eye, the star should appear to shift like my finger. I have carefully observed the positions of stars and have never found them to shift. If I can't observe such a shift, it doesn't exist. Hence Copernicus was wrong. That's why my system is superior to that of Copernicus. In my system the earth is still fixed at the center of the universe, in accordance with the

Scriptures, and the sun revolves in a circle around the earth. So far my system agrees with Ptolemy's. But now comes my master stroke, which brings us back to Copernicus. I set the planets revolving in circular orbits around the revolving sun, with Mercury and Venus in orbits that are smaller than the sun's orbit around the earth, and Mars, Jupiter, and Saturn in orbits that are larger than the sun's orbit."

Tycho smiled to himself as he thought of how cleverly he had avoided the "pitfalls of Copernicus and Ptolemy." But his smile was replaced by a frown when he thought of proving his theory. That was an entirely different matter. He couldn't do it, so he must convince Kepler of the correctness of the Tychonic system. Kepler would prove it for him.

As Tycho sat there half asleep, he began to play a game he often played when he was depressed or troubled. He would think of some experience in his past and try to recall every bit of it from beginning to end. He was quite good at this because he had such a remarkable memory that he hardly forgot anything. At the moment he was thinking about his uncle Joergen who had tried to persuade, in fact, to force the young Tycho to study law and statesmanship as "became the son of a Danish nobleman." But Tycho had stubbornly resisted. Tycho's father was governor of Helsingborg Castle near Elsinor when Tycho was born in the year 1546, and his uncle was a vice-admiral in the Danish navy. Uncle Joergen, who was childless, had kidnapped Tycho and raised him as his own son. At first Tycho's father had been enraged at this;

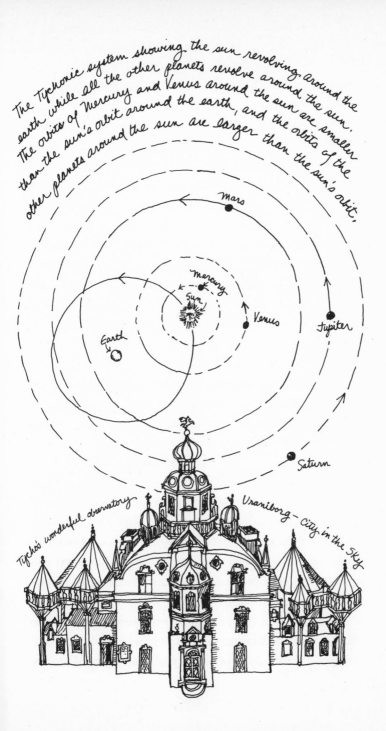

The Tychonic system showing the sun revolving around the earth while all the other planets revolve around the sun. The orbits of Mercury and Venus around the sun are smaller than the sun's orbit around the earth, and the orbits of the other planets around the sun are larger than the sun's orbit.

Mars

Mercury

Sun

Venus

Jupiter

Earth

Saturn

Tycho's wonderful observatory

Uraniborg — City in the Sky

later, however, he had calmed down and allowed his brother Joergen to adopt Tycho with the understanding that Tycho was to become either an admiral or a statesman.

This led to a test of wills between Tycho and his uncle, for Tycho had decided, by the time he was fourteen, that he would become an astronomer. When had this idea first occurred to him? Tycho turned his thoughts from Uncle Joergen to the two events that had influenced him. One occurred in his childhood and the other when he was about thirteen years old. As a young boy he often spent summers with his father at Helsingborg, which was built on a high peak overlooking the narrow sound that separates Denmark from Sweden. The sun set very late at Helsingborg during the early summer days, and Tycho had been given permission to sit up and watch it set every night. He was allowed to go to the very top of the castle, where the night watchmen were stationed, and from there he followed the fiery red disk of the sun as it sank below the horizon. He did this night after night, for he loved to watch the sky change gradually from twilight to pitch black, and to see star after star appear until there seemed to be hardly an empty spot anywhere in the sky.

In his third summer at Helsingborg, when he was eight years old, he observed an event that astonished him. During his two previous summers at the castle he had become familiar with the stars of the summer sky and knew which stars would appear first after the sun had set. He had also become aware of the patterns formed by the brightest stars. His tutor had told him that the ancient

Greek observers of the sky and stars called such patterns *constellations* and had given names of people and animals to them. There was Leo the lion, Ursa Major the great bear, Cancer the crab, Sagittarius the archer, and so on. Tycho could see nothing in the patterns of the stars that looked like men or beasts, but that in no way made them any less interesting and exciting. On this particular summer night he had watched the sun set as usual and was about to turn his gaze away from the western horizon when he detected a faint bright object just above the horizon and slightly to the left of where the sun had set. It soon disappeared below the horizon, but Tycho, young as he was, did not forget it.

He wondered all night and the following day whether he would ever see it again. The next night he had his answer. It was there again—and every night after that. By the end of the summer the object had moved so far to the left of the sun and was so far above the horizon that it could be seen for hours after the sun had set and it was so bright that all the stars he knew were faint by comparison. This object so stirred him that he could think of nothing more interesting than watching it. Later he learned that he was looking at the planet Venus. Now, dozing though he was, he smiled to himself as he saw that little boy standing at the top of his father's castle filled with wonder at the beauty of Venus.

The second event that drove everything but astronomy from his mind occurred one day when Tycho was fourteen years old. He was studying languages and philosophy at the University of Copenhagen where he had been sent by his uncle. He recalled the day very clearly. It was shortly after the noon hour and hundreds of people had collected in groups in the streets to watch the sun. They were waiting for an eclipse of the sun. Tycho had never seen an eclipse and was as excited by it as were all the others. But it was not the eclipse itself that excited him. It was the fact that it could be predicted. The idea that someone could say exactly when the eclipse would occur stirred him so deeply that there were tears in his eyes when the eclipse occurred exactly as predicted. The eclipse was only partial, and not very interesting in itself, but its occurrence amazed Tycho. To him it was "something divine that men could know the motions of stars so accurately that they were able a long time beforehand to predict their places and relative motions."

He wondered about it the rest of the day and deep into the night. "How can a person know the precise moment of an eclipse?" he asked himself over and over again. He finally realized that it could be done only if the "motions of the sun and moon from constellation to constellation were precisely known." It was clear to him then, young as he was, that it was all a matter of accurate astronomical observations and measurements. Indeed, he himself could make such predictions if he had the correct observations. He could then make predictions not only about the eclipses of the sun and the moon but also about the motions of the planets. He would know exactly where and when to look for Venus, Mars, and Jupiter. Since such knowledge was the basis not only of astronomy but also of astrology, he, Tycho, would become the greatest astrologer as well as the greatest astronomer of all time; and people from all over the world would seek him out. He had intoxicated himself with such ideas back there at Copenhagen, in those youthful days, but not for long. It was one thing to picture oneself a great astronomer and quite another to become one. His joy was changed to despair when he thought of how little he knew and how much he would still have to learn just to become an ordinary astronomer, let alone the greatest astronomer.

His natural optimism and his great self-confidence soon prevailed when he thought of how much he already knew. Though only fourteen, he could name every constellation and every bright star in the sky, and he knew through which of the twelve constellations—they were called Signs of the Zodiac—the sun would be passing each month of the year. He didn't know very much about the planets then, but he had discovered by himself that Venus returns to its same position on either side of the sun every 584 days. He was very proud of that discovery, which took him more than a year to make. How many other boys his age, or even grown-ups, for that matter, could have done that? He had watched Venus very carefully and patiently night after night. Others would have given up, but he didn't. That showed him that he had the necessary skill and patience to make precise astronomical observations. This cheered young Tyge considerably, but he knew how much he still had to do, and he made up his mind that he would do everything necessary to become an astronomer. He would read everything that had been written; he would study the sky more persistently than ever, and devote his time to star charts and to celestial globes.

Such were the thoughts and reminiscences that streamed through Tycho's mind as he sat at his table that festive night. Occasionally, as at this moment, he roused himself to see what was going on. Jepp had fallen asleep at his master's feet, the dogs were quietly curled up in front of the vast open hearth at the far end of the room, and the few remaining guests and the musicians were fast asleep. Tycho, assured that everything was quiet, went back to his reveries. Picking up his memories exactly where he had left off, he recalled how avidly and tirelessly he had thrown himself into the study of astronomy. For the remaining three years that he spent at the University of Copenhagen, he read every book on astronomy he could find, starting with the *Almagest* of Ptolemy and ending with Copernicus's *Book of the Revolutions.* At seventeen, happy with his ability to master such advanced books on astronomy, and having read them all, he knew that the time had come for him to begin astronomical observations in earnest. His uncle's wish that he become a statesman or an admiral meant nothing to Tycho who, shortly after this, was sent with a special tutor to study law at the great German university at Leipzig.

"You must make sure that Tyge gives up his foolish love of astronomy," Uncle Joergen had told the tutor, who was only four years older than Tycho. "Cure him of this illness and bring him back to the studies that are proper for the son of a nobleman. That will be your principal task."

Tycho now smiled to himself as he recalled how he had fooled his tutor. He had secretly bought a celestial globe and a cross-staff which he kept hidden under his bed. He studied the globe by candlelight, and when Vedel, his tutor, was asleep, he took out his cross-staff and carefully measured the positions of the stars and planets. Each time he made an observation of a star and determined its position, he compared it with the position of the stars given on the celestial globe. When he determined the position of a planet, he compared it with the position given in the planetary tables. When he did this for Saturn and Jupiter on August 17, 1563, when these two planets were almost at the same point in the sky, he was shocked to find that the planetary tables were in error by "a whole month." He saw then that his life's work was laid out for him. Very little that had been done in astronomy before could be trusted. All the observations of the planets that had been made up to then were worthless. He was happy and excited at the thought of what he had to do, and he went at it like a conqueror. He no longer hid what he was doing from Vedel, but carried on his work openly and with such fervor that he won Vedel over to his side.

As Tycho and Vedel went from university to university as student and tutor, Tycho's knowledge of astronomy increased to a point where he was considered more of a teacher than a student. His fame began to spread throughout Europe. He lectured wherever he went, at Wittenberg, at Rostock, at Basel and Augsburg, convincing all who would listen that very little about the heavens could be understood or explained without precise observations and accurate measurements of the stars and the planets. He also convinced them that he was the greatest astronomer of the age, the man who would bring precision to astronomy and change it from something to wonder about to an exact science.

And so it came to be. During the six years that Tycho spent traveling, studying, and lecturing in Germany, he designed and built the most accurate and largest astronomical instruments ever used up to that time. With these he made the most accurate observations of the planets and stars ever made up to that time. But this was just the beginning. He threw himself more and more deeply into his astronomical work, for he saw that astronomy could not be a part-time activity to be pursued occasionally. To achieve anything he would have to work at it every day and night. But to do this he would need a well-equipped observatory. When he returned to Denmark in 1572, at the age of twenty-six, Tycho began to plan the largest observatory ever built—large enough to house the enormous spheres, quadrants, and other devices he would construct.

But Tycho was still unknown in Denmark and could convince no one to give him an observatory, although another uncle, Steen Bille, gave him money for his instruments. Tycho would have to wait another four years before King Frederick II of Denmark, in 1576, recognized his genius and gave him the island of Hveen, lying in the sound between Copenhagen and Elsinor.

Before that happened, Tycho's name became known to young and old alike in Europe because of a remarkable celestial event that he was the first to discover. He recalled it now very clearly as he sat in the darkened dining hall reviewing his life.

It was on the evening of November 11, 1572—the very year he had returned to Denmark. The sun had set, and the moon was a thin crescent suspended above the western horizon. It was cold, very cold, and the air was so clear that Tycho could see things sharply for miles in all directions. He had spent the afternoon discussing alchemy with Uncle Steen, and he was hurrying home now, concerned that he would delay supper at the family estate at Knudstrup. Rushing along as he was, he still found time to look at the heavens. Looking at the heavens was to him like praying or reciting the rosary to a religious man. He had never lost his wonder at the beauty of the night sky, and the sky had never been as beautiful as it was that night.

Cygnus the swan, embedded in the Milky Way, hung above the western horizon; Orion the hunter had just risen; Taurus the bull with the seven Pleiades sisters was slightly to the west of Orion; Pegasus the winged horse was high above the southern horizon; and Venus, Jupiter, Mars, and Saturn were strung out along a line in the sky like pearls on a string. For a moment Tycho was overwhelmed with awe at this remarkable alignment of the planets which occurs so rarely. "As though God were showing me his handiwork," he thought to himself, as his eye followed the line of the planets upward to Andromeda, the Ethiopian princess. There his eyes stopped a moment as he wondered about the faint, hazy patch of light—like a tiny wisp of cloud—that marked the right elbow of Andromeda. It was neither a star nor a planet but some strange kind of celestial object that had puzzled astronomers for centuries. Tycho could only wonder at it, for he could no more explain it than could anyone else.

Shifting his gaze upward from Andromeda to her mother, Cassiopeia, the great W, almost at the sky's zenith, he stopped short in amazement. He could not believe what he saw, and for a moment thought he was dreaming or imagining things. There, slightly to the north of Cassiopeia, was an incredible sight—an extremely bright star that he had never seen before. It was brighter than Venus or Jupiter at their brightest. To convince himself he was not dreaming, and forgetting all about his supper, he ran from house to house calling on people to witness what was clearly a miracle—the birth of a new star. All who looked saw it and marveled at the star and at Tycho also, as though he himself had produced this "miracle."

It was more than an hour after Tycho had first seen the new star, or *nova*, as we now call such a star, that he went home. He was too excited to eat. Instead, he rushed to his quarters to study his celestial globe and star charts and to note the position of the nova as accurately as possible. He studied it all night, convincing himself that it did not move within the constellation and was, indeed, a star and not a planet or a comet which does move. The next morning he wrote to astronomers throughout Europe, calling their attention to the nova, which came to be known as Tycho's star. Within a month it had become so bright that people could see it in full daylight; then it began to fade, and it finally disappeared eighteen months later.

Those were heady, intoxicating days for Tycho. His fame had spread to Denmark, and even the king began to take notice of his famous subject. So it was that some three years later, in 1575, King Frederick, afraid that Tycho might remain in Germany where he was then traveling, decided to reward Tycho by deeding to him the island of Hveen. This was done in May 1576 when Tycho was thirty years old and at the peak of his intellectual and creative powers. "How wonderful, fruitful, and exciting those days were," thought Tycho now, as he pondered the twenty years that had passed since then.

He had ruled the three-mile-long island, which he had renamed "Island of Venus," with an iron hand. Maybe he had been too strict with his subjects and had demanded too much of his servants and assistants, but he had accomplished wonders in his famous observatory, Uraniburg, or "City in the Sky," as it came to be known. He had made astronomy an everyday occupation like farming or business. By observing the motions of the moon, sun, and planets every day of the year, for twenty years, he had made it possible for those who were to follow him to make precise astronomical predictions and to find the correct laws of the motions of the planets and the moon. Now, with his precise observations available to all who wanted them, the correct distances of the planets from the sun and their orbits could be calculated. The Ptolemaic theory could finally be proved or disproved; and if it proved to be wrong, as he knew it would, he was sure his own theory would replace it. That the heliocentric theory of Copernicus might be proved true, as indeed was done later by Kepler, never entered his mind.

Tycho thought of other things he had done. He had proved that comets move in orbits far beyond the moon's orbit, and he had remapped the sky and given the precise positions of a thousand stars.

Tycho was startled out of his pleasant dreams by Jepp, who had suddenly jumped up on the table and was dancing from one sleeping guest to the next, arousing each one by pulling his beard or knocking off his hat. Tycho roared with laughter at this strange sight and at the astonishment of the sleepers at their rude awakening. But Tycho's laughter stopped short as he felt the sudden sharp pains through his body. They had begun about six months ago and had become much more intense since then. He knew that an incurable disease was destroying him. The doctors had told him that he could prolong his life only by carefully controlling his diet and his drinking. But eating and drinking were among his greatest pleasures, and he paid little attention to the doctors' advice. He stuffed himself at every meal and washed down each mouthful with half a glass of wine.

But now he was losing more than his health—he was losing his beloved island and his observatory. The old king, Frederick, his dear friend, had died. The new king, Christian IV, had no love for Tycho or deep concern for his scientific work. Christian disliked Tycho's treatment of his subjects on Hveen and insisted that Tycho free the peasants he had imprisoned. He let Tycho know that all his revenues would be cut off if Tycho persisted in his high-handed ways. He had, in fact, already deprived Tycho of some of his income. Tycho was so enraged at this that he had decided to leave the island. "Let the young upstart try to get along without me," he thought. "We'll see how far he gets."

These thoughts comforted Tycho somewhat, but his eyes filled as he lumbered off to his chambers, knowing that this was the last banquet he would give and that princes would no longer dine at his table or pay him homage. His precious isle, so tied up with most of his life, was no longer his; his precious observatory and all his miraculous instruments would lie unused and moldering. Before falling off to sleep, just as the new day was dawning, Tycho began to have doubts about his great accomplishments.

"What have I really done?" he asked himself as he wondered whether his life had been in vain. "Who will carry on my work and prove that my theory of the motions of the sun and planets is right? Only Kepler can do it with his great mathematical skill. I must get him, above all, above all. There is much to be done, much to be done. In a week we shall all be leaving Hveen; leaving Hveen forever, forever, forever. . . ." And so Tycho fell into a restless sleep.

Michael had hardly finished reading the story of Tycho Brahe when his father entered the library and sat down at his desk. For a moment Michael found it difficult to return from Tycho and the Island of Venus to his father and the book-filled room.

As he sat in his chair, deep in thought, his father turned to him and said, "What is bothering you, Michael?"

"Nothing is bothering me, dad. I was just thinking that Tycho Brahe was a very strange man."

"Strange, Michael? What do you mean?"

"Well, I always thought scientists were modest and gentle people like Einstein. Tycho was a tyrant. He would have made a good pirate."

"One moment, Michael. Tycho was a person, and like all people a mixture of what we call good and bad. But the good in him far outweighed the bad. He was arrogant to people but humble before facts and uncompromisingly honest. He never lied about his achievements or took credit for anything he didn't do. He always gave full credit to others for their work. He could be cruel, but he was also gentle, generous, and kind. He was a loving father and loyal and dedicated to the mother of his children. She was a peasant woman and so, as a nobleman, he could not marry her; but he was never unfaithful to her and considered her his wife."

"You say he never lied about his scientific work, dad. Do you mean that there were scientists who did?"

"Yes, Michael, but very few, for which we can be thankful. Some scientists—again, very few—have taken credit for the work of others in their fields. But, on the whole, scientists are a very truthful bunch. At one time Tycho was sure a German astronomer, Reymers, had stolen some of his ideas, and a furious squabble went on between them until Reymers died. But there was no proof for that at all."

"Did Tycho finally get Kepler to work for him, dad? And why didn't Tycho see the stars shift back and forth every year as he said they should if the earth is revolving around the sun?"

"If you read on, Michael, you will learn what happened between Tycho and Kepler. As for your question about Tycho's failure to detect the yearly apparent motions of the stars as seen from the earth, the answer is that the effect is extremely small because the stars are so far away. As seen from the nearest star, Alpha Centauri, which is about four and a half light years, or twenty-six trillion miles, away, the orbit of the earth around the sun looks no bigger than the circumference of a dime does when viewed from a distance of about two miles. Tycho's mistake was in underestimating the distances of the stars. He was sure they weren't more than about sixty million miles away. He reasoned that, at that distance, the earth's motion around the sun ought to make them appear to shift back and forth annually by a large amount—large enough for him to measure with his naked eye. Knowing his own great observational ability, and not finding the annual shift of the stars, which we call the *annual parallax,* he rejected the idea that the earth moves. I suppose it was a kind of arrogance for him to think that if he couldn't detect something, it didn't exist."

"Can this shifting of the stars, the annual parallax, be observed and measured now, dad?"

"Oh yes, Michael. Very easily, with modern telescopes and modern photography. Measuring the annual parallax of the stars is the first step in finding the distances of the stars directly. But it was not until some two hundred and fifty years after Tycho Brahe's time that this was first done by the great German mathematician and astronomer, Bessel, who measured the parallax of a star in Cygnus. It took him almost three years to do it, and it was considered a great scientific breakthrough at the time. So you see, we can't blame Tycho for failing to observe such small motions."

With all his schoolwork and other activities, Michael didn't get back to the next chapter for some days, and when he did return to the manuscript, he found his sister reading it. She hadn't heard him enter the library, and he smiled as he saw how immersed she was in it.

Startled, she looked up somewhat guiltily as he called her name, but quickly became defiant. "Dad said I may read this, Michael, so don't—"

"But you won't understand it, Jessica."

"I *can* understand it. It's all written in English, isn't it? I can use a dictionary. I know how to use one and, anyway, even if I don't understand all the astronomy parts, I like the stories. I've just finished the story of

Aristarchus so you can go on reading where you left off."

With that she left, and Michael began reading the story of Kepler.

7·JOHANNES KEPLER: THE LAWGIVER OF THE SOLAR SYSTEM

The household at Benatek Castle, near Prague in Bohemia, had been in a turmoil for five days and nights. The priest, the doctors, his family and co-workers had been in constant attendance on the master, now writhing in pain, since he had returned, almost a week ago, from a festive supper at the estate of Baron Rosenberg. As usual, the master had consumed vast quantities of food and drink, and now he was suffering intensely from his overindulgence. On this, the fifth night of his illness, he had developed a high fever; at times he was delirious, not recognizing anyone, and repeating over and over again, "Let me not have lived in vain, let me not have lived in vain. . . ." During his lucid moments, he anxiously scanned the faces around him until his eyes fastened on those of a thin, dark-haired man at his bedside, who was studying the face of the dying man intently, as though trying to memorize every change in its features.

"Johann," whispered the sick master, grasping the hand of the man at his bedside and holding it tightly. "Johann," he implored, "you must promise—you must promise to prove that my theory is correct. My life will have been in vain and I shall not die in peace unless you do that for me."

"So this is how a great man dies, filled with doubt and anguish," Johannes Kepler thought as he watched the tortured face on the bed and leaned toward it to catch each word. The face looked so strange now with its heavy-lidded eyes and the tip of the nose missing. When the dying man stopped talking, Kepler spoke to him softly. "My noble master and most generous benefactor," he said, "My most noble Tycho, whom God has given to us that you might reveal to man God's heavenly mysteries. My dearest friend and mentor. My beloved guide and teacher, do not torture yourself with such doubts. No man has done what you have done, nor served God as you have. Your name will go down the ages and will never be forgotten. I thank heavenly providence that guided me to your doorstep."

These words seemed to reassure Tycho, whose life was rapidly slipping away. The seventeenth century was a year old, and Tycho Brahe was in the fifty-sixth year of his life; this was to be his last night. When Kepler finished talking, he was somewhat amazed at his own words and wondered whether he sincerely meant everything he had said to Tycho. He knew his own love of words and phrases and how easily he was carried away and used grand and flowery phrases once he began talking or writing about something in which his emotions were deeply involved. He knew he owed much to Tycho and that without Tycho's precise observations he would never complete his God-given task. But he wasn't sure he loved Tycho or was even fond of him.

He had been with Tycho at Benatek Castle for only a year; the year had had its pleasant moments but also its very stormy ones, for neither Tycho nor Kepler was an easy man to get along with. There had been quarrels between them, and Kepler had written abusive letters to Tycho when Kepler could not get from Tycho the observational data that Kepler needed for his work. Tycho was as jealous of the vast quantity of observational data he had collected as a miser was of his gold. He was most fearful that if he gave Kepler all his precious observations at once, Kepler would forget Tycho's theory of the solar system and devote himself entirely to proving the Copernican theory, which Kepler clearly favored. So Tycho doled out bits of information to Kepler during mealtimes as one might give stray bits of food to a begging dog.

During one of their discussions about what Kepler was to get from Tycho and how he was to work with Tycho, Kepler became so enraged at not obtaining Tycho's observations immediately that, in the words of Tycho, "he attacked me with the rage of a mad dog, to which animal he, Kepler, himself, so much likes to compare himself in irritability." At that moment in his life Kepler felt completely defeated and hopeless, for without Tycho's observations of Mars he could accomplish nothing.

In a state of despair, and filled with hate for Tycho, he left Benatek and rushed off to Prague.

"Let Tycho go hang himself" he thought. "I shall never work with him again." And to make sure that Tycho would know exactly how he felt, Kepler wrote another nasty letter to him swearing he would never return to Benatek.

Kepler thought of these things as he watched Tycho struggling for breath, and he felt deeply ashamed of the angry words he had hurled at Tycho during the past year. He knew now, as his sensitive, almost girlish features registered grief and his gentle eyes filled with tears, that he really loved and respected the dying man. He was glad now that he had not remained in Prague, away from Benatek, but had returned and written a letter of apology to Tycho in which he abused himself as much as he praised Tycho.

When Tycho had received this letter, he had rushed to Prague to forgive and bring the errant Kepler back to Benatek. But Kepler was no happier with the way things were between him and Tycho after he returned to Benatek than before he left. Tycho was as miserly with his observational data as before, and Kepler was at wit's end. It had been a miserable and unproductive year for Kepler; he wondered now, as he watched Tycho's life slipping away, what would happen to him when Tycho died. He began to feel as sorry for himself as he did for Tycho. Would this sorry state of affairs never improve? He wanted so little—Tycho's data—to achieve his goal, and that little seemed more difficult to get now than ever.

Things were pretty bad with Tycho alive, but Kepler did receive some data from him. If Tycho died, he might get no more of the precious data. Kepler had been excited and hopeful when he first came to Benatek, and now all that he had hoped for might be lost with Tycho's death. He was powerless to change things and could only wait.

At this sad moment it seemed to him that his whole life had been something of a misadventure—one tragic event and disappointment had followed another. Any person less passionately devoted to science and less driven by an intense belief that God had chosen him to discover the laws that govern the motions of the planets would have given up a long time ago. But Kepler was an incurable optimist with a need to fulfill what he considered his God-given purpose in life. That had kept him going. He tried to recall when he had first become aware of his interest in astronomy, but he couldn't push his memory back far enough. It seemed to him that he had always been interested although there was a period in his life when he appeared to be going in another direction.

Feeling the pressure of Tycho's hand grow weaker, Kepler, whose attention had strayed from Tycho, looked at him and was startled. He looked like Kepler's grandfather Sebald Kepler when he was dying. Grandfather Sebald had died six years ago—about two years after young Johannes had become a mathematics teacher in the Austrian city of Graz. Johannes, hearing that his grandfather was ill, had returned to his childhood home, to his grandfather's house in Weil-der-Stadt where he was born. It had changed little since his family had left it when Johannes was six years old. The room where his grandfather lay was darkened by the drawn shades, and Kepler with his bad eyesight had trouble seeing him clearly. When his eyes finally did focus on his grandfather's face, he was shocked at what he saw. Instead of the red, fleshy, full face with its arrogant look and angry eyes that he always remembered when he thought of his grandfather Sebald, Kepler saw a face on the pillow that was thin and pale with eyes that were barely open and unseeing. As Johannes looked at this strange, dying face, he thought of the six miserable years he had spent in that house.

"How frightened I was of my grandparents," he thought as he recalled the constant quarreling that went on between his mother and his grandmother. They both had the same name, Katharina, but they could agree about nothing and were always at each other. He recalled his grandmother as "restless, clever, and lying . . . slim and of a fiery nature; . . . vivacious—a troublemaker; jealous, full of hatred, violent, a bearer of grudges." His grandfather would often end the quarrels between his mother and grandmother by threatening to beat them both. He bellowed so loudly at the two women that Johannes, frightened out of his wits, ran off whimpering, to hide in some dark corner. It took him hours to recover from such experiences; even now, a grown man, he sometimes dreamed that his mother was being beaten by Sebald.

It had seemed to Kepler as a child that the Sebald household was in a constant turmoil, always noisy. He felt there was no one to turn to for love or comfort. How he had survived those early years he didn't know, for he was always sick and hardly able to stand. The worst time in his childhood had been when his mother had left him alone with his grandparents for a year. His father, Heinrich, who was "vicious, quarrelsome . . . a wanderer," and cruel to Kepler's mother, had run off to fight with the Spanish army in the Netherlands when Kepler was three years old. When his mother followed her husband shortly after that, Johannes felt completely abandoned and thought he would die; not until his parents returned a year later had he felt some happiness again. His grandparents had been unkind to him during that year and had treated him roughly. He also had contracted smallpox and had almost died before his parents returned.

Kepler had looked at his grandfather and known instantly that he was dying. Much as he had feared him when they had all lived together in that cramped house so many years ago, he now had only the tenderest thoughts for him. The room was almost filled with his relatives. They had all looked at him silently and respectfully when he had entered. They were proud of him, for he was the only one among them who had studied at a university and was now a teacher.

His grandmother Katharina had borne twelve children to grandfather Sebald, but only five of Johannes's eleven uncles and aunts were now alive, standing around their father's deathbed. Kepler knew they were a foolish, bungling lot, but he loved them dearly in spite of that.

Many of Johannes's cousins were also present, but he paid little attention to them—he was looking for his mother. He finally saw her standing near his grandmother, who was weeping silently and leaning against her shoulder. His mother had looked up when Johannes had entered the room. She was looking at him now with such sorrow and suffering in her eyes that Kepler could hardly hold his tears back. He felt guilty for having stayed away from her for so long.

"How wretched and unhappy her life has been," he thought as he approached her. "She has had comfort from neither my father nor from her children."

Johannes's father loved no one but himself and did little to support his family. As a boy, Johannes had feared him as much as he had feared his grandfather. In moments of anger, which were many, his father struck anyone who was near him, including his wife, which enraged the young Kepler. But Johannes was too frail and frightened to do anything about it. Heinrich Kepler was a restless wanderer who could not stay home for any length of time. Only warfare interested him. People said he would end his life on the gallows, which probably happened to him when he left home and disappeared forever when Johannes was seventeen years old.

Johannes had six brothers and sisters, but only three remained. His younger sister, Gretchen, was happily married, and his youngest brother, Christopher, was leading a fairly normal life as a pewterer. But his brother Heinrich was a misshapen being who had inherited his father's wanderlust and bad habits. He suffered from epileptic fits which made him unfit for any kind of work, and when his father threatened to sell him when he was fourteen, he ran off to Austria. After years of misfortune, he returned home half frozen to death. He had been bitten by animals, robbed and beaten by thieves, almost drowned, and very nearly burned alive. Heinrich was standing near his mother now, hardly aware of what was going on, his eyes downcast. Johannes felt sorry for him and knew that he would have to care for this brother as long as he lived.

He quickly walked over to his mother and kissed her tenderly and then looked deeply into her eyes as though to reassure her of his great love and trust. Kepler knew that she was a very suspicious woman whom many people feared because they thought she practiced witchcraft.

Regardless of what people said and thought about her, Johannes was deeply attached to his mother. The few moments of happiness he had experienced as a child had come through her, and she had given him his first feeling of excitement about the heavens and an interest in astronomy. It had happened in 1577 when he was six years old and a comet had appeared in the eastern sky shortly after sunset. It was the very comet whose orbit Tycho had tried to calculate. Everybody spoke about the comet that year—even Kepler's parents—and Johannes asked so many questions about it that his mother took him to "a high place to look at it."

Johannes never forgot the beauty of the sky that night. Everything he saw filled him with wonder and awe. In addition to the comet, the planets Venus and Jupiter were visible, and these three objects made a deep impression on him. For years after that he often recalled that event and how he and his mother had climbed the hill at one end of the town of Leonberg where they had moved after his father and mother had returned from the Netherlands. The sun had set, and as they walked along, hand in hand, beneath the trees that hid the sky, Johannes wondered what he would see. Suddenly they were at the top of the hill on an open plateau, and the entire sky was visible. His mother had been humming a strange tune as they walked along, but now she knelt beside him and pointed to the sky above the western horizon. There Johannes saw the comet with its long tail, with Jupiter and Venus below it. As he looked at these heavenly objects, star after star appeared in the sky. It grew darker until stars were everywhere and the sky was a glittering dome.

Three years later, when he was nine years old, his mother had shown him another remarkable heavenly event—an eclipse of the moon. What impressed him most about it was the way the color of the moon changed just before it was totally eclipsed. It had changed from its usual yellowish color to a deep red. This had puzzled Johannes for the rest of his life, for he never discovered why this change of color happened.

Johannes recalled these events as he comforted his mother and grandmother and watched his grandfather Sebald breathe his life away. As the day wore on and night approached, Johannes sat down at his grandfather's desk and took a small journal from his pocket, which he began to scan carefully. Pages of it had already been covered with Kepler's own writing, and it was clear from what he had written that he was keeping a record of events in his life. He had begun doing this when he was twenty-five years old, and it now contained many revealing things both good and bad about himself and members of his family. Johannes turned to the first page, which began:

On the birth of Johannes Kepler I have studied the events of my conception, which took place in the year 1571 May 16, at 4:37 A.M. . . . I was born premature, at thirty-two weeks, after 224 days, ten hours. . . .

At age four I almost died of smallpox, was in very ill health, and my hands were badly crippled. . . . At age six I lost a tooth. . . . From ages fourteen to sixteen I suffered constantly from skin diseases, often severe sores, often from the scabs of foul wounds on my feet which healed badly and kept breaking out again. . . . At sixteen on April 4, 1587 I was attacked by a fever. . . . At nineteen I began to suffer terribly from headaches and weakness of my limbs. The mange attacked me. . . . Then a dry disease. At twenty the cold brought a long attack of the mange. . . . A disturbance of body and mind had set in because of the excitement of the Carnival play in which I was playing Marianne. . . . At twenty-one I went down to Weil and lost a quarter florin at gambling. . . .

He smiled as he read some of the confessions he had written down with such truthfulness, holding nothing back. He constantly wondered about himself and why he was who he was, but he never knew what drove him to write such things down. He had an amazing memory for details and, like Tycho, could recall almost everything that had happened to him. As he turned the pages of the journal, he came upon an entry that dealt with his troubles from the age of fifteen on, when he was at the seminary at Adelberg, studying to become a clergyman. As he reread the passage he had written, he recalled how miserable and friendless he had felt:

February, 1586. *I suffered very much and almost died of my troubles. It was because of my dishonor and because I hated my school fellows whom fear made me denounce. . . . 1587. Koellin became my friend; I was beaten in a drunken quarrel by Rostock; various quarrels with Koellin. . . . 1580. I was promoted to rank of Bachelor. I had a sinful, lying witness against me, Mueller, and had many enemies among my comrades. . . .*

Kolinus did not hate me, I hated him. He pretended a friendship with me, but always opposed me. . . . My love of pleasure and other habits changed Braunbaum from being a friend into an equally great enemy. . . . I did not mind the hatred of Seiffer because the rest hated him too, and I provoked him although he had not harmed me.

"How strange that I should have wanted to become a priest," he thought. "It is so far from my mind now, and yet when I was a boy it seemed quite natural and the right thing to do." When he entered elementary school in

Leonberg, his teachers were greatly impressed with his brilliance as a scholar and his great devotion to God. It was decided that he study religion. He remembered the quarrels between his parents that his schooling had caused. His father cared little about educating Johannes and insisted that he become a laborer; his mother, just as strongly, insisted that he go to school.

"Her courage saved me," he thought as he looked up at her and blessed her devotion to him. "But it still took me five years to complete the three elementary classes because, obeying my father, I spent two years working on farms."

After Johannes's father had left his family for good in 1588, Kepler's road to the university was open; he entered the University of Tuebingen that September. He constantly worried about what others thought of him, and when things went wrong between him and his classmates, he often blamed and criticized himself severely, just as he had when he was at the seminary in Adelberg.

Now he was rereading the page he had written about himself just before he had left Graz to visit his dying grandfather. Referring to himself as "that man," he wrote:

That man is in every way doglike. He looks like a little lap dog. His body is agile, wiry, and well proportioned. Even his appetites are doglike: he liked gnawing bones and dry crusts of bread, and he was so greedy that whatever he saw, he grabbed; yet, like a dog he drinks little and likes the simplest food. His habits were the same as a dog's. He always sought the love of others, depended on others for everything, satisfied all their wishes, never got angry when they scolded him, . . . He dislikes conversation, but greets visitors just like a little dog; yet when anything, however small, is taken from him, he gets angry and growls. He attacks wrongdoers—that is, he barks at them. He is spiteful and bites people with his sarcasms. He dislikes many people and they avoid him, but his masters are fond of him. He has a doglike fear of baths, tinctures, and lotions.

As he read this passage, he knew that few people could write about themselves as he had. "Everybody wants to portray himself in the most favorable light, but I must write the truth about myself. Only then can I seek the truth in nature," he told himself.

A loud, rasping sound came from the bed. He jumped up quickly and was at the bedside in a moment. His grandfather was struggling for breath; his face was contorted with the effort, but that didn't last long. In a moment everything about him seemed to change. His face grew smooth, and he smiled as he opened his eyes and looked directly at Johannes, who had placed his hand on his grandfather's forehead. A tremor suddenly passed through his body, and he was gone. Johannes was amazed at how quickly it had happened. "To be alive at one moment and dead the next," he said to himself. "What does it all mean? What do life and death mean?"

Kepler had never seen a person die before, and he could never forget his grandfather's dying face. That is why he thought of him now, six years later, as he stood holding Tycho's hand. "Will he go the way my grandfather went or will it be different?" he wondered. He felt ashamed of himself that he should be thinking about such things while the great man was dying. But Kepler was as curious about death as he was about everything else that happened around him, and he could no more keep from wondering about it than he could help wondering about the stars. As Johannes studied Tycho's face and listened to his delirious words, he uttered a prayer of thanks that he and Tycho had been brought together.

He knew it was foreordained although it had begun in a most unexpected and accidental way, just when Kepler had finished his religious studies at the University of Tuebingen and was prepared to become a priest. Not only was Johannes the top student in religion at the university, but he was also far ahead of everyone else in mathematics and astronomy. He had mastered the Copernican theory easily, and he knew it so thoroughly that he had no trouble defending it against anyone who questioned it. In fact, he had become an expert in explaining and defending the Copernican theory, using mathematics so cleverly that few dared dispute him.

In spite of his brilliant mastery of astronomy and mathematics, Johannes loved religion so much that he never thought of becoming anything but a priest. Imagine, then, his astonishment when, on his twenty-third birthday, having passed all his examinations for the priesthood, he was offered the post of mathematics teacher at Graz. Since the faculty of Tuebingen had recommended him most strongly for this post, he felt obliged to accept it, which he did. Thus did Johannes start along a road that was to lead him to astronomy, to Tycho, and to everlasting scientific fame.

Determined though Kepler was to become a priest, even when he went to Graz to become a mathematics teacher, he devoted himself unsparingly to his teaching duties. He turned his mind more and more to mathematics and to astronomy. Many things about the solar system puzzled him. He was sure that the Copernican heliocentric theory was correct, but there were questions about it that Johannes felt still had to be answered:

Why were there just six planets?

Did the planets really move in circles as Copernicus stated they did; and if so, why?

Why, then, did his calculations show that the sun is not exactly at the center of all of these circles, which would seem to be the natural state for it?

Why were the planets at their given distances from the sun and at no others? What rules governed these distances?

Why did the planets move as they did, each with a different speed around the sun and each with a different period? What rules governed these speeds and the periods?

On and on the questions went until Kepler thought his head would burst. Then, one day in his classroom, while drawing a geometrical figure on the board, he was struck by what appeared to him a most amazing discovery. Just as there are five spacings or intervals between the six planets, there are five regular or perfect solids in geometry, as proved by Euclid. A regular solid is one in which all edges are of equal length and all faces are of equal area like a cube or an equilateral pyramid. To Kepler's fertile mind, which was sure that a single set of laws governed all things in nature, the two fives could not be a mere coincidence but could mean only one thing: the five distances between the six planets must be related in some way to the five regular geometrical solids, for why else would there be just five of each? He never forgot the tears of joy or the excitement of that idea and how it spurred him on to lengthy and difficult computations to see how he could fit the five distances between the planets to the five regular solids.

"The delight that I took in my discovery I shall never be able to describe in words," he wrote. "I no longer tired of my work; I shied from no computation, however difficult. Day and night I spent with calculations to see whether the proposition I had formulated fitted the Copernican orbits or whether my joy would be carried away by the winds."

So clever was Johannes, then only twenty-four years old, that even though his idea was wrong, he managed to convince himself that the five regular solids can be arranged to fit between the planets. To do this he used the distances of the planets from the sun given by Copernicus, which were wrong. Kepler was so thoroughly persuaded by his own arguments and reasoning, which

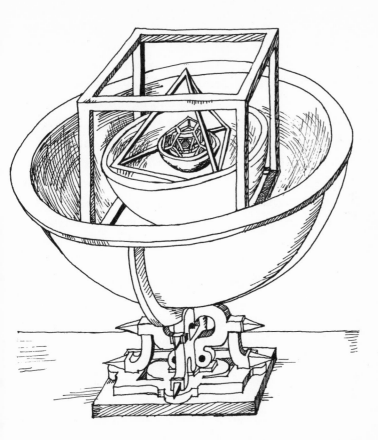

Kepler's incorrect construction of planetary orbits using regular solids. The outer sphere of Saturn circumscribes a cube which circumscribes the sphere of Jupiter. This in turn circumscribes a tetrahedron (4 faces) that encloses the sphere of Mars and so on. He assigned the dodecahedron (12 faces) to the earth, the icosahedron (20 faces) to Venus and the octahedron for Mercury.

were partly mathematical and partly religious, that he wrote a book about his theory called the *Mystery of the Universe.* The book, published in 1597, was written to praise God for having chosen him to "lift the veil which hides the majesty of God," and for having given him a "glimpse into its profound glory." "I was amazed," he wrote, "that precisely I, although a sinful person, had received this revelation, especially as I had not intended to enter the whole matter as an astronomer . . . but purely to amuse myself. In the event that I, as I believed, had correctly understood the matter, I vowed to God the All-Mighty and All-Merciful that at the first opportunity I would make public in print this wonderful example of his wisdom."

The book set the pattern for Kepler's life. After that, he said, "The direction of my whole life, of my studies and works, was set by this one booklet."

In the first part of his book Kepler tried to show how the Copernican theory agrees with religion and the Bible. But in the second part he carried out lengthy calculations to try to prove that the five distances between the planets could be related to the five regular solids. He did not succeed in this, but the agreement he did obtain between his calculations and the data given for the planets by Copernicus was close enough for some of the planets to convince him he was on the right track and had discovered the great secret of the universe. This, more than anything else, convinced him to become an astronomer. This was clear evidence that he had been chosen by God to become the discoverer of the laws of the universe.

Having sent his book to the outstanding scientists of the day, including Tycho Brahe and the great Galileo, Kepler prepared himself for the praise that he was sure would come to him and for offers of important positions from kings and heads of universities. But this did not happen, to his great disappointment. Those who read his book were greatly impressed with his cleverness. But men like Galileo pointed out that most of what Kepler had done was more or less brilliant guesswork. There were no real proofs. In time Kepler was aware of this, and saw that only if he could obtain precise planetary data could he prove the truth or falsity of his ideas. But where were the precise data to come from? He couldn't obtain these data himself, since he had no skill as an observer at all. These data could come from only one man, and that man was Tycho Brahe.

Kepler longed for Tycho even as Tycho longed for Kepler. Kepler expressed his longing in words: "Let all keep silent and listen to Tycho, who has given thirty-five years of his life to his observations. . . . For Tycho alone do I wait; he shall explain to me the order and arrangements of the orbits. . . . Then I hope I shall one day, if God keeps me alive, erect a wonderful edifice."

Johannes recalled these things as he stood at Tycho's bedside, waiting for Tycho to die. "How hopeful I was," he murmured to himself, "and how little progress I have made since then, for I still don't have what I need for my life's work. . . . I need Tycho's data on Mars. Once I work out the orbit of Mars, I shall have the answers to all my questions."

There had been many bitter and tragic days for Kepler between the time his book was published and the time he came to live with Tycho. He had married the daughter of a wealthy miller—a widow with one child. Though Kepler loved her and became very attached to his stepdaughter, his married life was miserable. His wife understood little of what he was trying to do and nagged him constantly about his lack of attention to her and his meager salary. He often blamed himself for their violent quarrels but could not prevent himself from speaking sharply to her when he lost his patience.

"I provoked her, and I regret it, for my studies sometimes made me thoughtless; but I learned my lesson, I learned to have patience with her. When I saw she took my words to heart, I would rather have bitten my own finger than to give her further offense. . . ."

The first child born to them—a son—died after two months. The daughter who followed died a month after her birth. These tragedies came at a time when Kepler was threatened with religious persecution because he was a Protestant and refused to give up his faith. He had the choice of becoming a Catholic or being driven out of Graz. It was just at this time, when Kepler saw no hope for completing his work at Graz, that he received the call from Tycho. So, on September 30, 1600, expelled from Graz, without any money, sick with fever and with a bad cough, Kepler took his wife and stepdaughter to Prague and then to the castle of Benatek.

A year had passed since then—a fruitless year for Kepler—and now Tycho was dying. As Kepler watched

Tycho's feverish face, he wondered if the emperor Rudolph II would allow him, Kepler, to obtain Tycho's data and continue his God-given work. Kepler received his answer two days after Tycho's magnificent funeral. On November 6, 1601, the emperor's privy councilor, Barwitz, informed Kepler that he had been appointed Tycho's successor as the imperial mathematician of Prague and that all Tycho's observations would now be available to him. This gave Kepler everything he had hoped for, and he set to work immediately calculating the correct orbit for Mars. He was to remain at this task for eleven years at Prague.

Mars was the key to the solution of the solar system problem. Venus posed no problem because its orbit is so nearly circular that Kepler had no trouble fitting it into the Copernican theory. But Mars was different, behaving like a spoiled child that refuses to obey the rules followed by the other members of the family. Kepler felt as though he were entering a battle with a real foe when he began to work on Mars, which he referred to as "that mighty victor over human curiosity . . . who kept the secret of his rule safe throughout all past centuries and followed his course in unrestrained freedom." Using Tycho's precious observations on Mars, he planned his attack on the planet carefully, calculating its orbit step by step.

The task was prodigious, and Kepler spent five years of intense work at it. At the end of that time, in 1606, his calculations, carefully arranged in small script, covered nine hundred pages. Out of it came a book called *The New Astronomy* dedicated to Emperor Rudolph II. In this book, which appeared in 1609, Kepler stated the first two of his three famous laws of planetary motion. This was really the beginning of modern astronomy and science. For the first time in history precise statements about the motions of heavenly bodies were made which could be precisely verified.

When Kepler began his epic calculations on Mars, trying to find a circular orbit for it that would fit all of Tycho's observations, he was sure he would succeed, for he had complete faith in Copernicus. But as his calculations progressed, he began to have doubts. No matter where he placed the sun, which Tycho's data showed could not be at the center of the orbit, he could not make the orbit circular. It turned in too much at some points and too little at others, no matter what he did. It was a question of either giving up circular orbits or doubting Tycho's data. But he could not doubt Tycho because, as he said, Tycho was "an accurate observer" given to mankind by "divine kindness" and "it is fitting that we should acknowledge this divine gift and put it to use." So Kepler gave up circular orbits.

Even then it took him some time to get the right answer. He saw soon enough from the data that the orbit of Mars was oval shaped, but that is as far as he got for quite a while. "Why an oval and what kind of oval?" he kept asking himself over and over again. "There are so many different kinds of ovals that I shall never find the correct one," he thought. Then he discovered something quite remarkable about the orbit of Mars which immediately gave him the answer he was seeking.

He first traced out the orbit of Mars to scale on a piece of paper using Tycho's data and placed a point at the correct position inside the orbit to represent the sun. He then found that a straight line drawn from the point of the orbit closest to the sun, which he called the *perihelion* of Mars, to the point on the orbit farthest from the sun, which he called the *aphelion* of Mars, passes through the sun itself. In other words the perihelion, the sun, and the aphelion lie on the same straight line. He measured the distance of the sun from the center of this line and then placed a fourth point on the line as far from the center of the line as the sun was, but on the other side of the center.

Now came his great discovery. He took a piece of string exactly as long as the line itself and pinned down one end of the string at the point of the sun and pinned down the other end at the fourth point on the line. He then found that if he hooked the piece of string around a pencil and kept the pencil tight against the string as he moved it, the point of the pencil on the paper traced out the orbit of Mars exactly. This told Kepler that the orbit of Mars is an ellipse, for Kepler knew all about ellipses. This means that if one takes the distance of Mars from the sun and adds to this the distance of Mars from the fourth point on the line drawn by Kepler, the sum is the same no matter where Mars is in its orbit. This sum equals the total length of the line from perihelion to aphelion. This is known as *Kepler's first law of planetary motion.* This law applies to all the planets. Each planet moves around the sun in its own ellipse. The points

Tracing out the orbit of Mars, Kepler found that
the orbit is an ellipse. If a string of length
PA is taken and one of its ends is pinned at the
position of the sun S and the other end at F, a
pencil that holds the string
taut will trace out an
ellipse. The sun and the
point F are equidistant
from the center C
and both of them
lie on the
line
connecting
the perihelion
and the aphelion.

pin

pin

P

C

A

Perihelion

S
Sun

F

Aphelion

occupied by the sun and the fourth point on the line are called the *foci of the ellipse.*

Kepler was amazed at his discovery, but also greatly puzzled by it. Although he knew about ellipses, he had never seriously considered them as planetary orbits. "I felt as if I had been awakened from a sleep," he said, when he first found that the orbit was an ellipse. He went on, "I thought and searched, until I went nearly mad, for a reason why the planet preferred an elliptical orbit. . . . Ah, what a foolish bird I have been!"

While Kepler was struggling with the shape of the orbit, he also wondered about the changing speed of Mars as it moved around the sun. He knew from calculations he had derived from Tycho's data that the closer Mars got to the sun, the faster it moved. In fact, when Mars was closest to the sun, at its perihelion, its distance from the sun multiplied by its speed was exactly equal to its speed multiplied by its distance when it was farthest from the sun, at its aphelion. But this is true only for the perihelion and aphelion distances. This almost led Kepler to the discovery of the law of gravity, for he reasoned that Mars is directed along its orbit by some kind of force from the sun. When the planet is closest to the sun, the planet moves fastest because the sun's force on the planet is then greatest. The sun's force decreases as the planet recedes from the sun, so that the planet's speed also decreases. But Kepler did not think of the sun's force as a pull toward the sun. He thought of the sun's action as though it were a broom pushing the planet from the side. That is where he went wrong and missed discovering the force of gravity.

But in thinking about the changing speed of Mars as it moves in its orbit around the sun he discovered the second law of planetary motion. He found that the line drawn from the sun to Mars sweeps over the same area during the same time no matter where Mars is in its orbit. This is known as *Kepler's law of areas*, and it applies to all the planets just as the first law does. It is sometimes stated by saying that the line from the sun to a planet sweeps out equal areas in equal times.

In spite of these remarkable achievements and his discovery and explanation of the basic optical principles of lenses and telescopes which occurred at about the same time, when he heard of Galileo's telescope, Kepler was not having an easy time of things. He had all kinds of minor official duties to perform which kept him from his great work, and he was constantly quarreling with Tycho's heirs about the ownership of Tycho's data.

Though his fame had grown and he was known and revered everywhere in Europe as a great scholar, Kepler and his family were still quite poor. His pay was low, and often he had to wait weeks before receiving it. This gave him an intense feeling of insecurity and brought on a constant fear of poverty. How would his wife and children survive, he asked himself over and over again? To add to his troubles his wife was often sick, and he suffered from real and imaginary ailments of all kinds. He felt miserable and doctored himself constantly.

So the years passed in Prague with Kepler struggling to

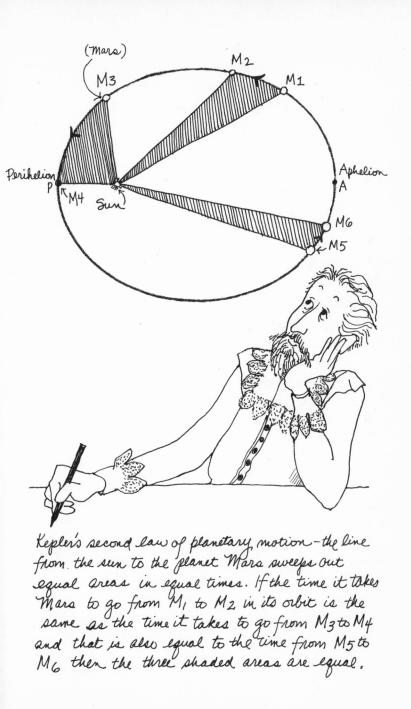

Kepler's second law of planetary motion — the line from the sun to the planet Mars sweeps out equal areas in equal times. If the time it takes Mars to go from M₁ to M₂ in its orbit is the same as the time it takes to go from M₃ to M₄ and that is also equal to the time from M₅ to M₆ then the three shaded areas are equal.

keep himself and his family well while his fame grew. But in 1611 tragedy struck him and his family. The old emperor, Rudolph, was deposed by his cousin Leopold, and civil war broke out in Prague. With the war came disease and pestilence; Kepler's wife, Barbara, and his three children contracted smallpox. The oldest and youngest child got well, but his wife and his favorite child, six-year-old Friedrich, died. Grieving over their deaths, Kepler took his two remaining children to Linz, Austria, where he was to remain for the next fourteen years as mathematician. This was a rather minor position, but he retained the title of imperial mathematician that he had received from the Emperor Rudolph in Prague.

Kepler knew that the two laws of planetary motion that he had discovered while in Prague did not give the total picture. The most important discovery had yet to be made. He had to find the relationship between the time it takes a planet to go around the sun and its distance from the sun. He was sure that some kind of grand harmony, stemming from God himself, ruled the planets. But what was it and how could he discover it? Kepler devoted six years of his life to this problem, trying out every idea he could think of. Finally, on March 8, 1618, he discovered what is now called *Kepler's third law*. It is also called the *harmonic law* because, to Kepler, it expressed the great harmony in the universe which he had been seeking since his youth.

All Kepler's suffering and misery were forgotten in the joy of his great discovery; it made everything—all the anguish—worthwhile. Now nothing could daunt him. Neither war nor illness nor fear of poverty.

"In vain does the God of War growl, snarl, roar, and try to interrupt with bombardments, trumpets, and all his madness," he wrote. "Let us despise his barbaric cries . . . and awaken our understanding and longing for the harmonies."

Kepler explains his third, or harmonic, law in a book he finished on May 27, 1618, *The Harmony of the World.* Describing how he had gradually arrived at the law and how he felt when he discovered it, he wrote:

What I predicted 22 years ago; what I have sought the last 16 years; that for which I joined Tycho Brahe and for which I settled in Prague; for which I have devoted most of my life, I have now discovered.

Having seen the first signs of dawn eighteen months ago, the light of day three months ago, but only a few days ago the unclouded sun in all its wonder . . . nothing shall now hold me back. I freely give myself up to sacred madness. I openly defy all mortals with this honest confession: I have stolen the golden vessels of the Egyptians to build with them a tabernacle for my God. . . . I am writing a book . . . for posterity. . . . It may wait a hundred years for a reader, since God also waited six thousand years for a discoverer.

In arriving at his third law, Kepler tried all kinds of numerical combinations of the "period" of the planet—

the time it takes the planet to revolve around the sun—and its mean distance from the sun, which is just half the major axis of the planet's orbit. After many numerical trials he finally discovered that if the period of the planet is multiplied by itself (this is called *the square of the period*), and if this product is then divided by the mean distance multiplied by itself twice (*the cube of the mean distance*), the resultant number is the same for all planets. Another way of saying this is that the squares of the periods of the planets are proportional to the cubes of their mean distances from the sun.

Even while Kepler was discovering this law and writing his book on cosmic harmonies, he was beset by troubles. The worst of these came when his mother, who still lived in Leonberg, was put on trial for witchcraft. This was a very serious charge. In the year 1615 alone—the year Kepler's mother was accused—six people in Leonberg were burned at the stake as witches. Kepler had great reason to fear for his mother's life, and he did all he could to save her. He prepared a very skillful defense and acted as her lawyer. After a trial lasting six years, during which she spent eighteen months in jail and was threatened with torture, she was acquitted of the charge and freed. Six months later, she died. Kepler's daughter Katharine died the year he finished his book.

Only one bright spot lightened Kepler's personal life during these trying years. A year after settling in Linz, he decided to remarry. He went at this project just as he went at his scientific work. He made no quick choice of a wife but considered eleven different candidates, weighing one against the other very carefully. He finally accepted number five, Susanna Reuttinger, the twenty-four-year-old daughter of a cabinetmaker. The marriage, which lasted from 1613 until Kepler's death on November 15, 1630, was a happy one. Seven children, three of whom died in infancy, were born to the couple.

After he published *The Harmony of the World*, Kepler went back to the task for which he had been hired by Emperor Rudolph: to complete the planetary tables that Tycho had begun. Kepler had been urged to do this from all sides. The tables were needed by astronomers, navigators, calendar makers, and astrologers. Kepler had put them off in words that tell exactly how he felt about tedious calculations: "I cannot work in an orderly manner, or stick to a pattern or to rules. . . . I beg thee, my friends, do not make me give all my time to mathematical computations . . . leave me time for philosophical speculations, which are my only delight."

Nevertheless, he finished the tables in 1624, and they were finally published in September 1627. They were used constantly for more than a hundred years after that.

During the last three years of his life, Kepler became very restless. He traveled about looking for peace, quiet, and financial security. These remained out of his reach to the end of his life. He died in the town of Ratisbon at the height of the Thirty Years' War, and was buried there on November 19, 1630. Today nobody knows where his grave is. The cemetery and the grave were destroyed by the war and nothing remains but the few words he had written for his gravestone:

I used to measure the heavens
  now I measure the shadows;
My soul was from heaven, my body lies here.

When Michael finished reading the story of Kepler, he felt that something wonderful had happened to him. He often felt like this when he heard a great piece of music or saw a great painting. But this was the first time he had felt this way about any person. What an amazing and gifted man Kepler was—as much a poet as he was an astronomer. How sure he was that he would discover the truth about the motions of the planets. It was clear to Michael that in spite of all the harsh things that Kepler had written about himself, he was the gentlest of men. Only a gentle person could have gone through all the troubles that had befallen Kepler and have remained without bitterness to the end.

Michael left the library wondering about Kepler and about how he had discovered his three laws of planetary motion. He felt that, compared to what Kepler had done, the work of Copernicus and even of Tycho Brahe had been quite simple, almost child's play. In the days that followed he spoke to his teachers about Kepler, and was surprised to learn how little they knew about him, as though he were some minor historical figure instead of an intellectual giant.

8 - THE MOONS OF JUPITER AND THE PHASES OF VENUS

The old man, kneeling in full ecclesiastical robes, was listening to the dull, unfeeling voice; but he was paying little attention to the words that drifted across to him from the stage where his judges sat. The day was extremely hot—the first day of summer—but the coolness of spring still lingered in the large hall. The old man had been brought there—to the hall in the Dominican Convent of Santa Maria Sopra Minerva in Rome—by a courier of the Inquisition. He was to hear the sentence which the Inquisition had imposed upon him. The hall was crowded. In addition to the cardinals and prelates of the church, many other important members of Roman society were there. Most of them had come out of curiosity—to see how the famous Italian scientist would react to his sentence.

He looked around him from time to time, but he recognized few people. He knew most of them, both friends and enemies, but the lighting in the hall was too poor for him to see their faces clearly. For weeks the cataract in his right eye had been growing steadily worse, and now hardly any light could get through it. He could still see with his left eye, but because of some kind of recent infection it kept filling with tears so that things were blurred. It didn't matter. He knew who these people were and had contempt for most of them—an ignorant, bigoted lot who thought they could undo discoveries and knowledge or stem the flow of ideas by a proclamation. "There is no hatred as great as ignorance's hatred of knowledge," he thought. "So be it, but knowledge will prevail over ignorance in spite of what these fools say or do."

The proceedings seemed endless. The voice went on and on. Some of the words sank into the old man's mind even though he was thinking of other things: "Whereas you, Galileo . . . of Florence, aged seventy years. . . ." They were right about that. He was seventy, to be sure, and his years had on the whole been exciting and happy ones. They could never take that away from him, nor could they stop what he had begun. He tried to recall the events that had started him on his scientific career. He wasn't sure when it had begun because as far back as he could recall, he had always wanted to find out about things. As a child he was either taking things apart or putting them together, and his greatest joy was to build toy machines for his younger brother, Michelangelo. They rarely worked, but that didn't matter.

Music, art, languages, and religion also excited him in those early years. To lie on the floor of his father's room in Pisa, where he was born, and to listen to his father play the lute was his greatest delight. In fact, the first thing he could remember in his life was his mother's singing him to sleep while his father accompanied her on the lute. His father was a clever man and skillful mathematician who wrote very learned papers on music and other subjects, but he was a poor merchant who barely earned enough to support his family. In spite of that, their lives were filled with joy, for his father never allowed anything to disturb their happiness. The young Galileo found pleasure and excitement in everything.

As the kneeling Galileo recalled his happy, carefree boyhood, some of the other words coming from the man on the stage struck him and interrupted his thoughts: ". . . for maintaining correspondence . . . with some German mathematician; also for publishing certain letters on the sunspots." He smiled at this stupid reference to Kepler—"some German mathematician." Not to know of his great discoveries showed their ignorance. He was glad he had not encouraged Kepler to come to Italy, for he too might have been caught by the Inquisition. And the "sunspots." Were they going to hold that against him also, he wondered? All they had to do was look through his telescope to see for themselves that the spots were there and that they moved as the sun rotated. He had begged them to look through the telescope, but they had refused saying that it was an instrument of the devil, who would make them see whatever he wanted them to see. Well, let them die in their ignorance if they were too stubborn to learn.

He lost track of the speaker's words. Again he was recalling his early years. His father had taken him to the famous monastery of Vallombrosa near Florence to perfect his Greek and Latin and to study logic. He remembered the breathtaking beauty of the valley in which the monastery sat. He had just turned fourteen, and he and his father had set out from Pisa on horseback early in the morning. As they rode along, his father talked in a gentle voice about many things, and everything he said aroused Galileo's desire. Whether it was music or art, poetry or mathematics, language or history, he wanted to study it. He wanted to know and master everything. He felt unhappy that he could not decide what he wanted to do most, and yet he was strangely excited. He knew that, somehow or other, a moment would come in his life when the choice would be made for him. There would perhaps be some kind of heavenly sign that would point the way for him.

It was well past noon that day, so long ago, when Galileo and his father entered the mountain pass that led to Vallombrosa. They had stopped for more than an hour to have their lunch near a mountain stream shaded by enormous oaks and maples. The boy was enchanted by everything around him. He was overwhelmed by the grandeur and beauty of the forest, and felt at that moment that he would want nothing more in his life than to devote himself to the service of God. During the rest of the trip, Galileo was silent and in deep thought. His father, sensing that his son had undergone some strange experience, studied him carefully. He was well aware of the great influence wielded by the church and how powerfully it could attract so sensitive a mind as his son's. He decided to keep in close touch with Galileo while he was at Vallombrosa and remove his son if there was any sign that he might be turning to the church.

When they came to Vallombrosa, the sun was setting; its golden rays made the entire valley look like a magic garden. Again Galileo was overwhelmed as he saw the tower of the monastery at Vallombrosa and heard the solemn and rapturous chanting of the monks preparing for their evening prayers. Again he was wonder-struck and engulfed by a deep religious feeling.

Galileo remained in Vallombrosa for about two years, and he now recalled longingly the carefree, lovely days there. How sweet it was to pass the time in the beautiful gardens surrounding the monastery. There he would play the lute to the accompaniment of the wind in the trees, or he would write poetry praising God and extolling the beauty of nature. At times he would lie in one of the fragrant meadows thinking about the world and the heavens, or spend a day painting some appealing scene. He had fallen so deeply in love with the place that he had about decided to become a monk when his father, fearful of the religious influence on the boy, withdrew him from the monastery. An entirely new life began for him.

As the kneeling Galileo thought now of these things, he was reawakened to his present plight by the words coming from the stage: ". . . and whereas thereupon was produced the copy of a letter . . . written by you to your pupil in which, following the hypothesis of Copernicus, you include several propositions contrary to the true sense and authority of the Holy Scriptures. . . ." There it was! They were accusing him of teaching the Copernican doctrine. But he had never really taught it in public. He had been very careful about that because he knew how dangerous these fools could be when they got it into their heads that their religious beliefs were being attacked or even threatened. How lucky Kepler was to have the freedom to say and teach what he wanted. Maybe he, Galileo, should have been more careful about what he said in private to his friends and his students. But he had spoken and written to many students. One of them was a traitor, perhaps even a spy sent by the Inquisition to trap him. He went over their names in his mind, but found none that he could not trust. "Yet one of them revealed the letter I sent him," he said to himself softly.

Of course he had vigorously supported the Copernican theory to his friends, and had pointed out its great superiority over the Ptolemaic theory. But the most he had done in his public writings and lectures was to point out that, taken as "a pure mathematical hypothesis," the Copernican theory had definite advantages over the doctrine of Ptolemy and was far simpler than Ptolemy's. To be sure, he had written and spoken publicly about all the discoveries he had made with his telescope and had indicated that they favored the Copernican theory far more than they did the Ptolemaic theory, which fixed the earth at the center of the universe, but he had always stuck to the facts.

"But facts mean nothing to these knaves," he murmured to himself. "They accept only the Scriptures as though the Scriptures contained all the secrets of the universe. But they no more understand the Scriptures than they understand my mathematics."

He recalled the letter he had written to his friend, the mathematician at Pisa, Father Castelli, in 1613. In the letter he had argued that the Scriptures should not be used to support or attack any natural law. "Who can assure us that everything that can be known in the world is known already? . . . This, therefore, being granted I think that in discussing natural phenomena we ought not begin with the Scriptures but with experiments and demonstrations for the Scriptures and Nature do alike proceed from the Divine Word."

It seemed at the time to be an innocent letter. But he was sure now that the Inquisition had got hold of it and would use it against him. He knew that Professor Castelli had circulated it widely, as he should have, and that it had been sent to the Inquisition by a certain Father Lorini, a bitter enemy. But how could anybody object to it? There was nothing in it that attacked the church, and it said nothing in favor of the Copernican theory. "But what difference does it really make?" he asked himself bitterly. "If they want to destroy me, they can do it however innocent I may be. If I can be accused of heresy just for describing what anyone can see through my telescope, nothing I say can save me."

These thoughts flashed through Galileo's mind in but a few seconds, and again he was recalling his early years. Coming home from Vallombrosa was like awakening from a beautiful dream, but he had little time to think about that. Before he could decide whether he wanted to be a teacher of languages, a musician, or a painter, he was sent off to the University of Pisa to study medicine—a very honorable and lucrative profession in those days. Somewhat unhappy at first, the young man soon realized that the university was where he wanted to be. He loved to investigate things and argue about everything, and there was no better place to do this than at one of the Italian universities where no one dared venture beyond the ideas of Aristotle and Plato, the ancient Greek philosophers.

"What exciting days those were," he mused. "Great discoveries were to be made everywhere if one just wanted to look. But the fools at the university didn't want to look. They just believed without question what Aristotle had written." He smiled when he thought of the violent arguments he had gotten into with students and professors alike. They called him "the Wrangler" because he let nothing go by without questioning it, and he soon made enemies of classmates and teachers. But he cared little about that, for he was also making important scientific discoveries. Each discovery filled him with amazement and drove him to make others.

"They began to take notice of me when I discovered the principle of the pendulum and showed them how it can be used to make a clock run accurately. They didn't argue with me then," he thought. While sitting in a church one day, he had observed that the rate at which a chandelier hanging above him was swinging back and forth (the period of the swing) was the same whether the chandelier was swinging in a large arc or in a small one. He later discovered that the rate of swing depends on the length of the swinging object. A long pendulum swings more slowly than a short one. "I had to beat them over the head with my ideas before they were even willing to listen to me." It all seemed amusing and unimportant now, but there was such anger then that he almost came to blows over some of his ideas. He had learned then that the best way to get along was not to push his ideas too strongly but to feed them to people gradually. But he was so impatient in those days that he could hardly restrain himself.

And then a remarkable thing happened to the young Galileo which turned him completely away from medicine and toward mathematics and physics. He overheard a mathematician by the name of Ricci teaching a student Euclid's geometry. Galileo was so struck by what he heard, for the teaching of mathematics was sadly neglected in Italy in those days, that he remained rooted to the spot until the geometry lesson was over. He then begged Ricci to teach him geometry also, to which Ricci consented. But Galileo, who was nineteen at the time, was to remain at the University of Pisa only one more year. The university refused to continue his scholarship after his third year because he was "not respectful of authority" and "too hostile to his teachers." Since his father was too poor to support him at the university, Galileo left and returned to Florence where his family was then living. Fortunately, Ricci was a good friend of Galileo's family, so he continued to tutor Galileo in mathematics at home.

Recalling these events now, as his sentence was being read, he smiled at the idea that he was "hostile to his teachers." To call such people teachers was a joke. All they knew was what they had memorized from books written centuries ago. He never regretted that he had openly shown his contempt for them, even though doing so had lost him his scholarship. He was suddenly struck by the similarity between his position then and now. Except that now he might not only lose his livelihood but his life. He wondered what they would do to him. They would certainly not act rashly or injure him. He was an internationally famous scholar and scientist; to harm him would shame and degrade the church in the eyes of the world. Thus reassuring himself, Galileo again turned his attention to what was being read. He could see that his sentence was being read by Cardinal Ascoli, whom he knew only by sight. "Does he really believe what he is reading?" Galileo wondered, as the words came to him:

"The proposition that the sun is in the center of the world and invariable . . . is absurd, philosophically false, and formally heretical because it is contrary to the Holy Scriptures.

". . . that the earth is not the center of the world nor immovable is also absurd, and false. . . .

"Should you refuse to give up altogether these false doctrines, as ordered by the Commissary of the Holy Office, and should you continue to teach them to others and to defend them . . . you shall be imprisoned."

So that was it, thought Galileo. Unless he denied everything he considered the truth, everything he had spent his life discovering, he would spend the rest of his days in prison. What a way to end his life! "Should I choose truth and jail, or a lie and freedom?" he wondered. "Why is it," he asked himself, "that our lives are always controlled and arranged by others?"

Even in those exciting years when he was at Florence discovering the great beauty of mathematics and physics under the guidance of Ricci, he was not free to do as he wanted. His greatest pleasure would have been to spend his days discovering the secrets of nature and proving theorems in geometry. But that was out of the question. He had to help support his family, and so he gave private lessons in mathematics and mechanics to students in Florence and the nearby town of Siena.

But in spite of that he was happy then, for everything seemed possible to him. One discovery followed another, and his fame began to spread among the well-established scholars and scientists of that period. Regardless of his scientific successes, Galileo found it almost impossible to earn a living. Having mastered most of what was known about mathematics and physics in those days, he felt he was prepared to teach at a university and so applied for a professorship in mathematics at various universities as vacancies occurred. He applied, in turn, to the universities of Bologna, Rome, Padua, Pisa, and Florence. But he was turned down each time.

After two years of fruitless effort he was so bitter that he had about decided to leave Florence and settle in Venice when the professorship of mathematics at the University of Pisa again fell vacant. This time, at age twenty-five, Galileo was appointed to the professorship at the miserable salary of 60 scudi, or 65 dollars, per year. That the appointment was to be for only three years and that his wretched salary was too small even for his food didn't matter. He was a professor at a great university! To be sure, he would have to do private tutoring on the side to earn enough to live on, but he would have ample time to carry out all his experiments and pursue his mathematics. That was what counted.

"No one could have been happier than I in those days," he thought, as the remembrance of those events came back to him now. It had become quite warm in the hall in which he was kneeling before the Inquisitors, and his penitential robes weighed heavily on him. Hoping it would all end soon, he again turned his attention to the words of the speaker: ". . . that so pernicious a doctrine might be . . . rooted out . . . the Holy Congregation of the Index shall prohibit the books which treat this doctrine, declaring it false. . . ."

Ignorant fools, to think that ideas can be declared true or false by edict instead of by careful scientific experiment. From the day he had gone to the University of Pisa as professor of mathematics, he had been badgered and attacked by fools. At Pisa they threw the words of Aristotle at him, trying to ridicule his experiments on the motions of bodies. They were like fleas annoying a lion and in no way stopped him from going on with his experiments.

One important discovery followed another. He was amazed that nobody before him had thought of challenging Aristotle's false assertions by simply watching the way bodies actually move. Why, he wondered, had nobody before him thought of just dropping two stones, one heavy and one light, from the same height and actually observing, as he had done, that they both fall to the ground at practically the same speed? The slight difference in their speeds was clearly due to the air resistance. This simple experiment revealed a very important law of nature: that the rate at which the speeds of freely falling bodies increase (the acceleration of gravity) is the same for all bodies in a vacuum. Having no vacuum to work with, Galileo used very dense small bodies to minimize air friction. In a vacuum, a pound bar of gold and a grain of dust would fall equally fast with the speed of each one increasing by exactly the same amount in each unit of time. Since this contradicted Aristotle, students and professors alike had refused to listen and had derided and laughed at Galileo.

But nothing could stop him. He went on to show that all Aristotle's ideas about motion were wrong. By allowing metal spheres to roll down an inclined plane, which he could adjust to reduce their speeds to any desired amount, he measured the acceleration of gravity and found that the speed of a freely falling body increased by 980 centimeters per second every second. He timed the rolling body by humming a tune at a definite beat. Contrary to what Aristotle had written, Galileo found that a force is not required to keep a body moving at constant speed along the same straight line. The only reason that bodies like a rolling ball or an object sliding along the ground don't go on moving forever by themselves is that the force of friction between the ground and the body resists the motion and stops them. If there were no friction, objects would go on forever because of their own inertia. They would not have to be pushed along or pulled by a force. In fact, force has nothing to do with speed; it is related to acceleration. One had to apply a force to a body only if one wanted to change its speed, the direction along which it was moving, or both speed and direction.

Galileo was amazed at the anger and hatred these ideas of his provoked at the university. People came to his lectures more often to hiss and cause disturbances than to listen. He stood up to these challenges and attacks with remarkable courage, but that only enraged his opposition even more.

With his pay so low that he could not support himself, and with the attacks against him growing more violent and more frequent, Galileo decided to give up his professorship at Pisa. He returned to Florence, hoping that he would be offered the mathematics professorship at the University of Padua, which was then vacant. He had had his eye on the position at Padua for a long time, not only because it was a larger and more liberal university than Pisa, but also because the pay was better. But he was turned down when he first applied for the position.

He remembered now how disappointed he had been and how difficult things were for him at that time. He adored his older sister, Virginia, who was married in 1591, the year that he left Pisa, and he had spent every cent he could scrape together to buy her a wedding present. "It was a silken bedcurtain," he whispered to himself as he recalled how beautiful she looked in her wedding gown. "I bought the silk in Lucca and had special silk fringes made to adorn the curtains and the bedstead." He could see her now, hugging him with delight when he brought her the present. "And enough silk was left over to make four or five vests for my father and my brother Michelangelo. But it left me penniless."

The first great tragedy in his life struck him that very year. His father, who had set him along the path of so many wonderful and exciting adventures, and whom he loved so dearly, died, leaving him to support his mother, his brother, and his two younger sisters. He also had to supply the dowry for his sister Virginia. He was desperate at this point in his life and knew that his only hope was Padua. Without Padua, he and his family would drown. He could not bear to see the anguish in his mother's eyes or to see how frightened his sisters were at the thought of poverty, so he buried himself in all kinds of activities. Not being able to carry on his scientific work in the way he wanted to, he turned to writing. He wrote furiously. He wrote all kinds of things—poetry, plays, critical essays, and philosophy. Anything to keep his mind off his troubles. He had applied to Padua again and was again rejected. Then, when he had just about given up hope, he was appointed to the professorship at Padua after his third application.

"How different things were there," he recalled. "I was treated as a great scientist should be and respected wherever I went. All doors were open to me, even those of the prince himself. Students and famous people from all over Europe attended my lectures." He tried to remember some of the great names that had come to learn from him: Archduke Ferdinand, emperor of Germany; the Landgrave of Hess; the Prince of Alsace and Mantua; Prince Gustavus of Sweden; and the famous English scientist William Harvey, the discoverer of the circulation of blood.

His lecture room was almost like a circus with its magnificent demonstrations and scientific wonders, and Galileo entered and departed like a great actor who always had the audience in the palm of his hand.

He had become famous throughout Europe because of his clever instruments and experiments which revealed one secret of nature after another. In quick succession he had invented the hydrostatic balance to measure the specific gravity of solids, the geometrical and military compass, the hydraulic lift, the air thermometer, the pendulum clock, and other devices. An expert writer, he had issued many pamphlets and books describing his work. No wonder, then, that at the end of his first four-year term at Padua he was reappointed for a second six-year term at about 400 scudi a year, almost twice his original salary.

But financial difficulties still plagued him. He still had his mother and his youngest sister to support, and he now had two dowries to pay; his middle sister, Livia, whose dowry Galileo had agreed to pay, was now also married. Virginia's husband was so enraged at Galileo because he had not paid her full dowry that he threatened to have Galileo imprisoned if he ever dared return to Florence. To add to these problems, Galileo had fallen in love with a Venetian, Lady Marina Gamba, who in the years 1600, 1601, and 1606 bore him two daughters and a son: Virginia, Livia, and Vincenzio, named after Galileo's father. To support his own family as well as his mother and sister was an enormous burden, but nothing could dampen Galileo's spirits. He was revered by all and was on the verge of his greatest scientific discoveries. He worked feverishly, day and night, as though driven by a constant hunger. People marveled at his energy and tireless activity.

"And this is what it has brought me," he murmured as his attention again turned to the words condemning him: ". . . the title of which showed that you were the author, which title is *The Dialogue of Galileo Galilei, on the Two Principal Systems of the World—the Ptolemaic and Copernican*. . . ."

They were condemning his book—the one he had published just a year ago summing up, in his most powerful and persuasive way, all his arguments favoring the Copernican theory and all those opposing the Ptolemaic theory. Having learned of Kepler's work and his laws of planetary motion, he was more certain than ever that the heliocentric theory was correct.

He had written the book in the form of a conversation among three friends, one of whom supports Aristotle and Ptolemy, one supports Copernicus, while the third is impartial. He had made the supporter of Aristotle and Ptolemy appear foolish and unable to withstand the clever arguments of the Copernican and the sly, biting wit of his impartial friend who favors Copernicus. Galileo had written the book in ordinary Italian instead of the usual Latin, the academic language, because, as he said, "I wish everyone to be able to read what I say." Referring to Latin as "gibberish," he went on to say, "I see young men brought together to study . . . medicine, philosophy . . . who have a decent set of brains . . . but being unable to understand things written in gibberish . . . think that there must be some grand hocus pocus of logic and philosophy to jump at. I want such people to know that as Nature has given eyes to them just as well as to philosophers for the purpose of seeing her works so she has given them brains for examining and understanding them."

Thus Galileo attacked the blind worship of authority and threw down the gauntlet to those who were hanging on to the dead past. At the same time he firmly stated his faith in the simple folk around him. This didn't sit well with the "high and mighty," of course, and when people all over Italy began devouring and applauding Galileo's book, it was clear that he would be challenged by the church. The book was considered not only an outstanding work of science but also, by many, a great literary satire in which the rather simple, foolish supporter of Ptolemy was thought to portray the pope, while the clever supporter of Copernicus was thought to be Galileo himself.

"Of course I didn't mean that at all," he said to himself now. "I hold the pope in greatest esteem. But what does it matter? They wanted to persecute me and the book was the excuse they needed." He suddenly recalled the words of Father Ricardi, the censor, who had attacked him quite openly when the book was published and had stated that "the Jesuits will now persecute Galileo with utmost bitterness." And now he was, indeed, being bitterly persecuted.

Again he became aware of the words of his persecutors: ". . . in consequence of the printing of the said book, the false opinion of the earth's motion and stability of the sun is daily gaining ground. . . ."

So even the Inquisitors were aware that more and more people were turning away from Ptolemy and turning to Copernicus. What they didn't know is that nothing could ever reverse this move to Copernicus. Things might have been different if the telescope had not been invented and if he, Galileo, had not built one and looked at the heavenly bodies with it. How amazed he was when he first viewed the moon with the telescope—and then Jupiter, Saturn, Venus, and the Milky Way itself! What wonders were revealed to him! Never had he been so thrilled and excited as when he saw the four moons of Jupiter and the stars in the Milky Way. Thousands and thousands of stars, like grains of sugar on a dark tablecloth.

Galileo took pleasure in thinking of those days when he astounded everyone in Venice with his telescope. It happened during his seventeenth year at Padua. He was forty-five years old and well established as the most famous professor there. He had left Padua for a day to visit some friends in Venice. They were greatly excited by the news that a Dutchman had invented a spyglass which made distant objects appear larger and closer.

"What do you think, Galileo?" they had asked him. "Is such a thing possible?" He gave a cautious answer which left them wondering.

All the way home he thought deeply about the problem, and by the time he got there, he saw the solution. He had never thought much about optics, but he saw that to construct a telescope, all he had to do was to place one piece of clear glass with properly curved surfaces (called a *lens*) at one end of a hollow tube and another kind of lens at the other end. The trick, as Galileo saw it, was to make the front lens thicker at its center than along its circumference, but to make the back lens, the lens through which the eye looks, thinner at its center than along its circumference. A front lens of this sort would cause all the rays passing through it to converge and form an image. The back lens, or eye lens, would then conduct the rays into the eye. Galileo

Galileo's Telescope

the front lens or objective is convex and the back lens or eyepiece is concave.

arranged two such lenses, one convex and the other concave, precisely in this way, and it worked beautifully.

He succeeded in constructing a telescope which brought distant objects ten times closer and made them appear ten times larger than they would do to the naked eye. News of the Galilean telescope spread like wildfire through Venice, and crowds of people came to the university to see it. But Galileo had taken the telescope to the palace of the grand duke to whom he presented it as a gift. On leaving the chambers of the duke, Galileo was informed by the head of the university, who had been invited to attend the meeting with the duke, that the Senate had voted to appoint him to his professorship for life and to raise his salary to 1000 florins a year, which is about 1200 dollars.

Galileo was overjoyed at this, but what excited him more than anything else was his plan to look at the heavenly bodies with his telescope. That would settle many matters about which there were bitter arguments. He had already taken a quick glance at the moon with the first telescope he had built, but he did little more than note that the surface of the moon was quite rough and looked like the surface of the earth. This first telescope was just not good enough to show him all he wanted to see. Working tirelessly, he built one telescope after another until he had what he wanted—a telescope that brought distant objects at least fifty times closer. This was the key that unlocked the door to the secrets of the universe, and Galileo gave "thanks to God who has been pleased to make me the first observer of marvelous things unrevealed to bygone ages."

Each new discovery was more wondrous than the one before. After noting the rough, irregular surface features of the moon which "was a body very similar to the earth," he turned to the Milky Way and saw that it consisted of thousands of stars. This settled the question as to the nature of the Milky Way about which philosophers had been arguing for hundreds of years. He then discovered the sunspots and the rings around Saturn, which he first mistook for two moons. But to Galileo "the greatest marvel of all" was his discovery of the four moons of Jupiter which he referred to as "four new planets revolving around another very great star [Jupiter] in the same way as Mercury and Venus, and . . . the other known planets move around the sun."

Galileo was jubilant. That was all he needed to convince him that Copernicus and Kepler were right. But more definite and more convincing proof was to come some time after he had left the University of Padua to become first mathematician at the University of Pisa and philosopher to the grand duke of Florence.

At that time he turned his telescope toward Venus. He was amazed to see that, unlike Jupiter, Venus did not show up as a bright disk in the telescope, but rather with changing crescent shapes like the moon. In fact, its shape changed all the way from a thin crescent to almost full. This meant that Venus could not be revolving in a small epicycle between the earth and the sun, as demanded by

the Ptolemaic theory, because it would then always lie
between the earth and the sun as the moon does at
crescent phase. If that were the case, it would always
appear like a crescent because only a small piece of it
would then reflect light to the earth. To go from a
crescent shape to almost full before it was lost in the
bright light of the sun, as Venus did, meant that it moved
in an orbit around the sun that lies between the sun and
the earth. This is the only way Venus could be in a
position with the sun between it and the earth so that its
full face could be seen. There was nothing more to argue
about. The evidence in favor of the Copernican theory
was so overwhelming that anyone willing to look through
his telescope could be convinced immediately. But few
who opposed the Copernican theory were willing to look,
and the very evidence that Galileo thought would bring
people to his side was being used by the Inquisitors to
condemn him.

Saddened to the point of tears at his present plight,
Galileo looked around him now and was aware that the
final moment for his sentencing had come. A painful
silence had settled over the hall.

Cardinal Ascoli, who had stopped reading and was
looking directly at him, began to read again: "Invoking
the most holy name of our Lord . . . We pronounce this
our final sentence. We declare . . . that you . . . Galileo
are guilty of heresy. . . . To be pardoned, at Our
pleasure, you must, in Our presence, reject, curse, and
detest all your errors and heresies . . . contrary to the
Catholic Church of Rome.

The various phases of Venus as seen through a Telescope on earth. In position 1 only a small crescent AB can be seen. In position 2 the visibible portion of Venus AB is much larger. In positions 3 and 4 the visible portion AB is almost ½ of Venus' surface. In position 5 Venus is invisible from the earth.

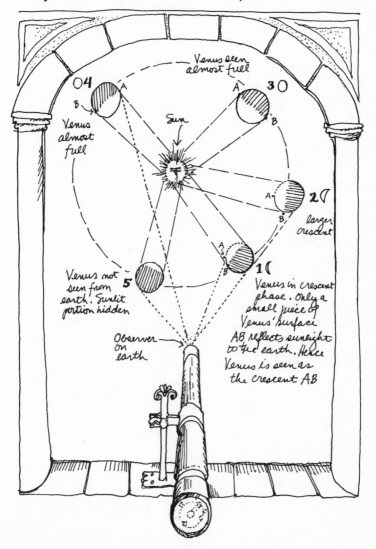

Venus seen almost full

O 4   A
B →
Venus almost full

Sun

A   3 O
B

A ·   2 ☽
B
larger crescent

A   1 ☽
B

Venus not seen from earth. Sunlit portion hidden   5

Venus in crescent phase. Only a small piece of Venus' surface AB reflects sunlight to the earth. Hence Venus is seen as the crescent AB

Observer on earth →

". . . that you be made more cautious in the future and as a warning to others . . . we decree that the book *Dialogues of Galileo Galilei* be prohibited by a public edict . . . We condemn you to the formal prison of this Holy Office for a period determinable at Our pleasure. . . ."

What was he to do, he wondered. Should he stand up boldly and denounce the Inquisitors and the entire proceedings or accept the sentence and reject his own beliefs? For a moment he thought of rising and challenging their right to judge him. But suddenly such weariness settled over him and his legs felt so weak that he could only remain on his knees with his head bowed. He remained there for some minutes while the throng was hushed.

Then, in a low voice, he began recanting his beliefs, reading from a page that had been handed to him: "I, Galileo Galilei . . . aged seventy years . . . swear that I have always believed every article which the Holy Church of Rome holds, teaches, and preaches. . . . I reject, curse, and detest the errors and heresies that I previously held; and I swear that I will never more in the future say or write anything to support what I now denounce. . . . I swear to denounce all who hold such heresies. . . . If I violate these promises that I now make let me suffer the pains and punishments decreed by you. . . ."

Though Galileo was not imprisoned and was allowed to retire, unguarded, to a small villa near his beloved Florence, his sorrows were not ended. He was happy at being near the convent where his two daughters lived as nuns, but he was overwhelmed by a sense of tragedy and of misfortunes yet to come. He loved to visit his daughters and was especially fond of the elder, Maria Celeste, who, he said, "possessed extraordinary mental gifts, combined with rare goodness of heart; and she was very much attached to me." He had always been concerned about Maria Celeste's health and felt that she was driving herself too much and undertaking tasks beyond her strength. She had written to Galileo, shortly before he was allowed to return to his small villa, that she prayed daily that she might live long enough to see him again, for she knew she would soon die. When Galileo finally arrived at the convent he saw that Sister Maria had fallen "into a profound melancholy which undermined her health." She died shortly after that, on April 2, 1634, at the age of thirty-four, leaving Galileo "in deepest grief." "I feel," he wrote, "that I am destined speedily to follow her, for I hear her constantly calling me."

Galileo did not die then, in spite of all his physical ailments and his grief, but lived on for eight more years. He was attacked by a severe fever on November 5, 1642, and died three days later—in the very year that Isaac Newton was born.

The last eight years of Galileo's life were very productive years. Despite his confinement by the Inquisition, he could go where he pleased and do what he wanted as long as he did not teach or defend the Copernican theory. So he continued the scientific investigations that had been interrupted by the Inquisition and completed many of them. These were all summarized in his last book, *The Dialogues on the Two New Sciences*, which was published in Amsterdam in 1638. His final year of life was a fairly happy one. Scientists from all over the world admired and honored him as their leader. Best of all, his family, his friends, and his students were in constant attendance. Their love and devotion soothed him and made him quite happy during the last few months of his life.

Michael had learned about Galileo in school and knew something about the troubles he had had with the Inquisition. But he was never quite sure what Galileo had done. Although his work with the telescope was very dramatic and changed the whole course of astronomy, Michael felt that Galileo's discoveries concerning the motions of bodies were more fundamental. This was indeed the case, as Michael later discovered in conversations with his father.

Before laying down the manuscript, Michael saw that only one more story remained. He would return to read it the next day.

9-HOW THE SUN CONTROLS THE PLANETS

If one had been living in the village of Grantham, England, in the spring of 1654, he might have seen a thirteen-year-old boy walk the length of the village each morning from a comfortable-looking white house to a red brick schoolhouse set among some beautiful old trees. The boy, a pack of books and school pads strapped to his back, never went directly to school but strayed into all the bypaths along the way, looking into every bush and listening to every sound. Occasionally he looked at the clouds in the sky, wondering about them and noting the direction of their drift.

This pattern never changed. Though the boy seemed to dawdle on his way, as though time and school meant nothing to him, he was never late. He always entered his classroom and took his seat quietly just before classes began and sat there, rarely saying a word. He spoke only when questioned directly, and though his answers were correct, they never quite satisfied the teacher, who thought the boy was shiftless and was shirking his schoolwork. He did, indeed, give that impression, for he hardly ever seemed to be paying attention to what was said in class. He seemed always to be daydreaming, his mind thousands of miles away from the schoolroom. This so annoyed the teacher that he had placed the boy at the very bottom of the class.

Isaac Newton, for that was the boy's name, cared little about his standing in class and even less about what his teacher and classmates thought of him. He was content with any rating they gave him as long as he was allowed to go his own way, thinking his own thoughts, and doing what he wanted to do. His classmates thought him rather strange and unfriendly, for he disliked the rough games they were always playing and he shared his thoughts with no one. He spent most of his time by himself reading, wandering around the lovely meadows, or tinkering with all kinds of tools with which he loved to build toys, knickknacks, and models of machines. He was fond of his classmates, but he felt that what they were doing was trifling and wasteful of time. He was sorry for them and wished he could do things for them and show them the way to more serious activities than their silly games.

Most of the boys in his class were not aware of Isaac's concern, for he rarely allowed anyone to know his thoughts. They simply looked upon him as a dull fellow, who was best left alone to his tinkering and daydreaming. A few resented him, for they thought he was putting on airs and considered himself too good for them. Since he stood near the bottom of the class, they could see no reason for him to feel superior.

Yet they were never quite sure he was as dull as he appeared to be. He had a way of making a remark every now and then during classroom discussions of some difficult problem that seemed to point directly to the answer. But he never allowed himself to say more than a few words. It was as though he were always standing guard over his thoughts and wanted nobody to get more than a glimpse of what was going on in his mind. They often would see him writing in a notebook that he carried around with him. They suspected that what he wrote in it had nothing to do with his schoolwork. He seemed to take notes at random, no matter where he happened to be. Occasionally they would find him in the schoolyard or out in a field observing the position of the sun and writing in his notebook as the sun moved across the sky.

One of their group had told them that one day, while passing Isaac's house, he had seen him drive a peg in the side of the house and then carefully measure the length of the shadow of the peg cast by the sun. He had walked over to Isaac, and when he saw many pegs on the side of the house, and some even on the roof, he had asked him what he was doing. Smiling gently, Isaac had told him he was making a clock. They all laughed when they heard this strange answer and thought that Isaac was probably slightly insane in addition to being dull.

In time, most of his classmates accepted Isaac with all his strange habits and even grew fond of him; but a few did not. Among these was an older boy who stood slightly above Isaac in class and took every opportunity to bully and annoy him. They sometimes met on the way to school. One morning the older boy, irritated by Isaac's disregard of him, began to punch and kick him. Completely unprepared, Isaac could hardly defend himself. Although he managed to ward off most of the blows, a particularly vicious kick caught him right below the chest and sent waves of pain through him. Frightened at what he had done, the older boy ran off. Isaac, barely able to walk and his eyes filled with tears, dragged himself to school.

He sat in his seat brooding all day, wondering what to do, and finally decided on two things. First, he would challenge the bully to a fight, and by beating him prove that he, Isaac, was the better fighter and was not afraid of physical conflict. Then he would prove to everyone that he was the better student by mastering all his studies. Isaac and the older boy fought that day after school in the churchyard, and Isaac won handily.

The day that followed was not a happy one for Isaac. It was one of those beautiful spring days that are found only in certain parts of England, and that morning the apple trees that lined the roadway along which Isaac walked to school were heavy with blossoms. Every few hundred yards the pink and white pattern of the apple trees was broken by cherry trees whose intense white blossoms hung like snow along the branches.

This was the time of year Isaac loved most, and he would have found the greatest delight in the beauty of the countryside that morning if he had not been deeply troubled by what had happened the previous day. To see anyone wrongly accused or mistreated almost made him ill, and it was only his anger that restored his sense of well-being. He could not bear to see anyone humiliated, least of all himself.

These thoughts, carefully marshaled as he walked along the footpath, eased his mind, for he felt he had behaved honorably and not from blind anger. He was justified in what he had done, and now he would show his classmates, and indeed the whole school, that he could surpass everyone in scholarly work. He would then invent special games, toys, and machines for his classmates that would teach them science and the pleasures of learning.

He began thinking about making a special kind of paper kite which, if properly designed, would rise with hardly any urging and would easily demonstrate the lifting action of the air. He was concentrating so intently on this problem, working out the details of the design in his head, that he failed to see that he had passed the schoolhouse and was walking through a meadow. He might, indeed, have walked right into a nearby brook if a pair of meadowlarks, whose nest he had disturbed, had not flown almost directly at him and broken his chain of thought. Startled for a moment, and concerned that he was late for school, he quickly looked at the sun. Estimating its height above the horizon, he was relieved to see that there was still a half hour to go before school began. He must have walked much faster than he usually did, as though his feet were trying to keep pace with his mind.

Looking around him, he was suddenly struck by the loveliness of the countryside and the fragrance of the meadow. All the sights and sounds combined to give him a sense of being part of a divine order in which everything in the universe played its special role according to precise laws. "The laws are God-given," he said to himself, "but they are precise, and man's role is to discover and understand these laws. That's what I shall do."

He felt instinctively and without any doubt that he *would* discover the laws of nature. He had great confidence in his ability to do just that because of the way his mind worked. It never gave up on a problem, and his powers of concentration were so great that nothing could distract him from his goal once he tackled a problem. As he said later in his life, his mind needed but the merest crack in what appeared to be an impenetrable wall, to pierce the wall and see what lay behind it.

Looking back at his boyhood, he recalled how his complete concentration on some particular idea often vexed his mother, who used to give him small tasks and send him on minor errands. Lost in thought on some problem, he often did not begin the task at all, without realizing that he was not doing his mother's bidding. And when it came to errands, he would start out as directed, but either return without having completed the errand or not return at all. On such occasions his mother would find him sitting under a hedge intently watching some insects or observing the ripples caused by pebbles dropped in a pond.

Isaac would look up at her with such remorse that, instead of scolding him, she took him in her arms, kissed him tenderly, and gently caressed him. Those were precious moments which he never forgot, as he could never forget how his mother looked at him, with a kind of wonder and with something akin to disbelief, as though she were not sure he was real.

In time Isaac knew why that was. His father had died before he was born, and his mother had given birth to him at the end of seven months, on Christmas Day, 1642. Not only was he a premature baby, but he was also so frail and weak at birth that the two women who attended his mother were sure he would die. He must have been no larger than a kitten, for his mother often told him that he could have been put "into a quart mug." Everybody loved his mother. She came from ordinary English stock, as did his father, and was known as a "woman of high character and fine intellect," who "employed her time educating her son and doing good works." Isaac was so frail during the first two years of his life that his neck was hardly strong enough to support his head. To help him keep it upright, his mother had made him a special collar which he wore when he was out of bed.

Isaac recalled his boyhood as he walked back slowly to the schoolhouse, quite determined to outdistance everyone scholastically. His mother would be pleased at that, for she had hinted from time to time that if he did well at Grantham School, she would arrange to send him to the university. She had married again, and Isaac now had a stepbrother and two stepsisters of whom he was very fond. It was a happy household. His stepfather, the Reverend Barnabas Smith, was a kind and gentle man who loved his stepson as much as he loved his own children.

At the end of Isaac's second year at Grantham, his stepfather died, leaving his mother with all the burdens of running a large farm and taking care of young children. Although her husband had left her fairly well off, she still felt that she needed help, and so, when Isaac was sixteen and had completed his fourth year at Grantham, his mother brought him home to help run the farm. She soon discovered, however, that her son would never succeed as a farmer, so she sent him back to Grantham for another year to prepare to enter Cambridge University. It was a quiet and happy year for the young Newton, for he was now respected and held in some awe by classmates and teachers alike. He was also in love. He had grown very fond of a Miss Storey, the lovely stepdaughter of the people he was staying with in Grantham. When he left for Cambridge University at the age of nineteen, they were engaged to be married. All who knew them praised God for bringing together two people so well suited to each other.

No wonder, then, that Isaac left home saddened at his separation from Miss Storey and unhappy at the thought of being at a large university with no friends and unknown to anyone. When he arrived at Cambridge he quickly learned that he was not at all well prepared to fit into the scholarly or social life there. He disliked the hurly-burly of university life which seemed always to intrude on his precious solitude. Nor could he get used to the constant disorder and lack of discipline that prevailed in the classrooms and lecture halls. Often the racket and noise where he lived were so great that he ran out of his rooms looking for peace and quiet. To make things worse, he had little free time because he was constantly running errands and doing other small jobs to pay for his tuition. So it was, during those early years at Cambridge, that he returned home whenever he could, to enjoy the companionship of his family and friends, but most of all, to read quietly or walk alone through the meadows.

Returning to Cambridge after such quiet vacations was painful to Newton, but in time he became more and more accustomed to the tumultuous life there. After his first two years, he rarely returned home. He had become so involved in the study of mathematics and science that he spent every spare moment reading books on these subjects and working out problems. More important, he thought up problems of his own and invented special ways of solving them. At the same time he began attending lectures on astronomy and optics, and he soon realized that very little about the way things behave in nature was really known. Many facts were presented by the professors, but knowledge of the facts alone didn't satisfy Newton. He had an intense desire to know why things happened the way they do and to find the underlying laws that relate one set of facts to another.

Just as at Grantham he had decided to outstrip everyone scholastically and had feverishly devoured every bit of knowledge he could, so now, at Cambridge, he threw himself into mastering mathematics and science. He read the books of Copernicus, Kepler, and Galileo which greatly stimulated his interest in astronomy. He was most excited by Kepler's *Optics*, which led him to the study of light, one of his favorite subjects, and to the design and construction of telescopes. He hardly had time to sleep or eat, so busy was he with his books, his inventions, and his observations. All kinds of questions kept him awake or stopped him dead in his tracks as he thought about them and tried to find answers. Why are there rings around the moon? In what kind of orbit does a comet move? Does a comet obey Kepler's laws of planetary motion? How is the motion of a body related to the force applied to the body? What causes the color in the rainbow?

He also began to design various instruments to study light. One of these consisted of two prisms so arranged that the colors coming from one prism could pass through the other. This enabled him to study how a prism affects light and led him to the important discovery that white light is a mixture of all the colors and that these colors do not come from the prism itself. At the same time he began to design a telescope in which a large mirror was used instead of a lens. The advantage of a mirror over a lens is that a mirror has no color errors, whereas a lens does. Moreover, it is easier to make a large mirror than a large lens. So engrossed was he in these enterprises that a year had passed since his last visit home. Now he was about to graduate from Cambridge, but an unhappy incident interrupted his work. He became ill. He had driven himself too hard and was forced to rest.

As he lay in bed fretting about his idleness and wondering how soon he could get back to his studies, he began to see that he had not been doing things in an orderly manner. He was trying to do too many things at once. There was no point in filling his mind with new facts and ideas if he didn't organize them properly and try to arrange them in some understandable pattern. Such thoughts soothed him and made it easier for him to bear his illness. Fortunately, the illness was not serious. He was strong enough to overcome it in time to prepare for his final examinations, which he passed without difficulty.

This was a very happy time for Isaac, who now found pleasure in the companionship of others. While ill, he had wondered how he could best arrange his time to do his best work and achieve his goals. He knew that if he concentrated hard enough on any problem, he could solve it; but now, with so many problems to think about, he didn't know which one would reward him most. He decided that the thing to do was to distract himself in some way, and then to open his mind to the problems one by one and solve each one in turn.

He spent a part of the summer of 1665 at Cambridge relaxing and organizing his ideas, hoping that he would have enough time in the autumn of that year to answer all the questions he had temporarily put aside. But he wasn't too sure of that. Autumn was a busy time at the university, and he hoped that he would be appointed to a teaching post in mathematics, which would take a great deal of his time. An event happened, however, that prevented him from returning to Cambridge and gave him two years of leisure. This was the time he needed to put his ideas in order and to make many of the great discoveries that were to make him famous and lead to his knighthood.

At the beginning of the summer of 1665, news had come to Cambridge from London and other large cities that the Great Plague, or black death, had broken out and was spreading rapidly. People in London were dying by the thousands, and all who could were leaving the English cities to live in the country. The authorities at Cambridge did nothing about this until early in August when they decided to close the university. Newton left with the others and returned to his mother's home in the secluded village of Woolsthorpe, where he lived alone and was free to do what he wanted and to think as he pleased.

This was a golden period in his life. Wandering undisturbed through the fields, deep in thought and watching the long, hot summer days give way to the cool days of autumn, acted on Newton like a tonic. After a morning of such wandering and concentrated thought he would return to the quiet house and fill page upon page with mathematical equations and very precise and careful reasoning. Later, in describing the many things he did during that free period, he stated that "all this was done in the two years 1665 to 1666, for in those years I was in the prime of my age for invention and minded mathematics and philosophy more than anytime since."

What were these great discoveries and accomplishments that now mark Newton as one of two greatest scientists of all time (Einstein being the other)? In mathematics, in addition to important theorems in algebra and geometry, Newton laid the foundation for differential and integral calculus. This is the basis of all modern mathematics and is the single most powerful analytical tool that mankind possesses. Without it, most of modern science would be impossible. In optics, as we have mentioned, he showed that all light consisted of primary colors, the colors of the rainbow, that cannot be broken up into other colors. In the realm of astronomy, he discovered the law of gravity and showed that the same force that causes an apple to fall to the ground keeps the moon moving in its orbit around the earth.

The magnitude of these achievements is so great that even today, after more than three hundred years, we are still amazed at it. How did it happen that Isaac, who showed no special promise as a boy and was no better at Cambridge than many others, suddenly at the age of twenty-three began doing such remarkable things, finally coming up with the law of gravity? We cannot say. But we do know that he was at his best when he was in the countryside and was allowed to go his own way in solitude. He did just that at Woolsthorpe.

For some time he had been wondering about the motions of the planets and why they moved in accordance with Kepler's three laws, but the answer to that question eluded him until one day in the fall of 1666. As was his practice, he arose early, ate a light breakfast, and walked slowly from the house toward the orchard. His favorite spot in the orchard was a small grassy area under some old apple trees where he always spent some time thinking about whatever problem he had on his mind. The delicious fragrance of the ripe apples that had fallen from the trees, the slight humming of the insects all around him, and the sighing of the trees seemed to lend wings to his thoughts. Everything seemed possible to him then. Problems that appeared to have no solution and that had bothered him for days seemed much easier when he thought about them there.

On this particular morning, looking up at one of the apple trees, he noted an unusually large ripe apple which seemed about to fall. He saw that it would take but the slightest pull to tear it from its branch. In thinking about pulling the apple from its branch, Newton was suddenly struck by a very exciting idea, and it came to him just as the apple fell from the tree by itself. It was a very simple idea and yet an overpowering one.

"Why," he thought to himself, "do we say that we pull the apple off the tree when we use our hands to remove it but say that the apple falls to the ground when it drops by itself? If it is correct to say that my hand pulls the apple, then it is just as correct to say that the earth pulls the apple. The apple falls to the ground not because all things have a natural tendency to fall but because it is pulled to the ground."

He looked up at the tree with its branches laden with

fruit and noted how the branches curved downward, as though each apple were being pulled toward the ground by a string extending to it from the ground. But there were no strings from the ground to the apples. How, then, could the ground pull an apple or, for that matter, anything else without touching it? Very strange, indeed. If the earth was pulling all things toward it, it was pulling them from a distance. That puzzled Newton very much, for he could not understand how one object could possibly act on another when the two were separated by empty space. This was so mysterious a thing that he almost felt like giving up the idea that the earth pulls things toward it.

But Newton didn't give up the idea. He reasoned that if action at a distance was mysterious, it was just as mysterious to have an object fall to the ground because falling to the ground was in the nature of the object. He did not know how the earth pulled on objects, but it seemed to him far more sensible to have an object fall because it was pulled than to say that falling is a part of its nature like hardness or color.

"To say that an object behaves in such and such a way because such behavior is part of its nature is to say nothing," Newton reasoned. "Moreover, to think of things in that way leads to nothing and blocks one from further progress. To introduce a force, however, is much more sensible and productive. We know how a force is related to the motion of a body. Galileo taught us that. If, then, we think of the earth as pulling objects toward it, it must also pull the moon and cause it to move the way it does. We should then be able to calculate the earth's action on the moon and thus see whether our contention is correct by comparing our calculation with the observed motion of the moon."

Isaac was so excited by this idea that he forgot all about everything else that he had planned for that morning. He could hardly wait to get to his desk and carry out the calculations on the motion of the moon. Even as he ran toward the house, his mind was at work trying to figure out exactly how the calculations were to be done. As he sat down and took out his pad and pencil, he saw that the problem was not nearly as easy as it sounded. He knew from the experiments of Galileo on falling bodies that an object in a vacuum falls toward the earth with increasing speed just as the falling apple did, even though the friction of the air hindered it a bit. He also knew from Galileo that such a freely falling object has a downward speed of 32.2 feet per second after the first second, a speed of 64.4 feet per second after the second second, 96.6 feet per second after the third second, and so on. In other words, the speed of a freely falling body on the surface of the earth increases by 32.2 feet per second at the end of each second.

Galileo called this rate of increase of speed the *acceleration of the freely falling body*. He discovered that all bodies in a vacuum, regardless of their weight, fall with the same acceleration. Galileo's experiments on moving bodies had also shown that a body can be accelerated only if it is pushed or pulled, that is, only if a force is applied to it.

Isaac was now elated, for things began to fall neatly into place. "If a force is needed to accelerate a body," he reasoned, "then it is clear that a body, such as a falling apple, that is accelerated must have a force acting on it. The apple was certainly accelerated when it fell from the tree because its speed increased steadily until it hit the ground. This means that a net force was acting on the apple as it fell. So far, so good. But we may deduce more than that. Galileo taught that the force acting on a body and the acceleration of the body are in the same direction—the acceleration is directed along the same line as the force. But we know that the acceleration of the apple is downward, along a vertical line. This means that the force acting on the apple, the force of gravity, is also downward. In fact, the direction of the force of gravity, being vertical, is toward the center of the earth."

It didn't take Newton long to come to the conclusion that the earth exerts a force—the force of gravity—on all things on its surface. It was also clear to him why the force of gravity stems from the center of the earth. (He couldn't prove this at the moment, but it seemed reasonable to him.) The earth was a sphere, and apples on trees all over the world would fall along vertical lines toward the surface of the earth. Since all these vertical lines meet at the center of the earth, as would the falling apples if the earth's surface didn't stop them, the force must behave as though it came from the center of the earth.

"How beautiful," he thought, "that God has invented such a simple and yet extremely efficient and effective way of preventing things from falling away from the earth. He made the earth spherical and then gave it the ability to attract all things to its center. How clever a solution to a very difficult problem! But then, one would expect that from God. This made it possible for ships to sail the oceans and for living things to walk upright everywhere on the earth without experiencing any change in their weight, for our weight is nothing more than the pull of the earth on each of us—the pull of gravity—which is the same wherever we may be on the earth. How wonderful gravity is! It tells us *up* is where our heads are and *down* is where our feet are, no matter where we are on the earth.

"But if the earth pulls apples to the ground from the branches of trees," he went on reasoning, "it also pulls rocks down the sides of mountains, no matter how high the mountains are. Even if a mountain were a hundred, a thousand, or ten thousand miles high, rocks free to move would roll down its side because of the earth's force of gravity. We may imagine, then, a mountain so high that its peak extends to the moon. If I let a boulder go from the top of such a mountain, that boulder would also roll down. Hence the moon itself must be pulled by the earth. But now I am faced with two questions that I must answer before I can test my theory against the observed motion of the moon. First, why doesn't the moon fall to the earth like boulders on mountainsides? Second, suppose I weighed myself at the foot of this very tall mountain and then weighed myself at the top; what would the difference be? Put differently, how does the acceleration of the apple falling from the tree on the earth compare with the acceleration of a boulder falling freely from the top of the very tall mountain?"

Newton found the answer to the first question quite easily. It had to do with two distinct motions of the moon. It was clear to him that the moon did not fall onto the earth, in spite of the fact that the earth was pulling it, because it was moving parallel to the earth's surface at the same time that it was falling toward the earth. It had a horizontal speed not influenced by the force of gravity, which is vertical. If one stood at the top of a mountain and simply dropped a stone, it would fall with increasing speed directly to the foot of the mountain. On the other hand, if one threw the same stone horizontally with a definite speed, the stone would fall vertically downward with increasing speed at the same time as it continued moving horizontally with the same unchanging horizontal speed with which it was thrown, since there was no horizontal force acting on it. Newton saw this at once and figured out quite easily the path it would trace out as it fell to the earth. It would, of course, strike the earth at some distance from the foot of the mountain. But the faster it was thrown horizontally, the farther from the foot of the mountain it would land.

It then occurred to him that if one could throw a stone horizontally fast enough, it would never land because the path taken by the stone would never curve enough for the stone to strike the earth. For this to happen, one would have to throw the stone fast enough in the horizontal direction so that its horizontal motion com-

Moon

A

B

C

D

E

Moon's orbit
around
the earth

Earth

the moon in its very
nearly circular motion around
the earth is constantly falling in
toward the earth owing to the earth's
gravitational pull. It does not fall onto the
earth because its circular motion consists of a
horizontal part AB (parallel to the earth's surface)
and a vertical part BC (toward the center of the earth).
In one second it moves a horizontal distance AB equal to
3350 feet. At the same time it falls a vertical distance
BC equal to slightly more than $\frac{1}{20}$th of an inch. If
the earth did not pull the moon it would continue
along the direction AB forever.

bined with its downward or vertical motion always kept it at the same height—the height of the mountain—above the earth. Newton saw at once that the moon was doing just that. It was falling toward the center of the earth all the time. But it always stayed at about the same distance from the earth because its horizontal motion was just fast enough to offset its vertical downward motion.

But how was he to use this to prove that the falling apple and the falling of the moon were both caused by the force of gravity from the earth? He had to do two things. First, he had to calculate from the observed motion of the moon how far it falls toward the center of the earth in one second and compare that with how far an object on the earth drops during the first second of its fall. Second, he had to find the principle or law that describes how the force of gravity decreases with increasing distance from the earth, and then see whether, from that law of decrease, he could calculate how fast the moon should fall in one second.

Newton tackled the second problem first. He reasoned that if the force of gravity goes out equally in all directions from the center of the earth, it spreads out more and more and must weaken with increasing distance. In the same way, the brightness of a candle sends out light equally in all directions and decreases with increasing distance. He knew the answer to that. He had learned long ago that if the distance of a candle is doubled, its brightness decreases fourfold; if its distance is tripled, it becomes nine times fainter; and so on. Its brightness falls off as the square of its distance. If, then, the force of gravity depends on distance in the same way as brightness does, the earth's force of gravity must be four times weaker at a distance of 4000 miles above the surface of the earth than at the surface of the earth, which is itself 4000 miles from the earth's center. A man standing on top of a mountain 4000 miles high would then weigh only one-quarter of what he does on the surface of the earth. On top of an 8000-mile-high mountain he would weigh only one-ninth of what he does on the earth because he would then be three times farther from the center, and so on.

Newton called this the *inverse square law of gravity.* Gravity falls off as the square of the distance.

If this were true, and Newton was sure it was, then the distance an object falls during the first second of its descent toward the earth, one-half the acceleration of the earth's gravity at that point, should change with increasing distance from the earth in the same way as the force of gravity or the weight of a person does. On the surface of the earth an object in a vacuum falls 16.1 feet during the first second. Hence, on top of a 4000-mile-high mountain, it should fall 4.02 feet in the same time (one-fourth of 16.1); on top of an 8000-mile-high mountain it would fall 1.8 feet during the first second (one-ninth of 16.1); and so on.

If this inverse square law of gravity were correct, he could then obtain the distance the moon falls toward the earth each second by first dividing the distance of the moon's center from the earth's center by 4000 miles and squaring the number so obtained, since that would be the

the second law

Illustrating how the force of gravity decreases with distance from the particle M. At the distance "d" the force is concentrated over the area ABCD. At twice the distance (2d) the force is spread over the area A'B'C'D' which is four times larger than ABCD. At three times the distance (3d) the same force is spread over the ninefold area A"B"C"D" which is the square of 3.

square of the moon's distance from the earth. What he would have to do after that would be to divide this last number into 16.1, and the answer would be the distance, in feet, the moon falls toward the earth every second. He could change this into inches by multiplying by 12, and twice this would be the earth's acceleration of gravity at the distance of the moon.

Hardly had Newton figured this out than he began the calculation. Since he knew, from his studies of astronomy, that the moon's distance from the center of the earth is 60 times greater than the earth's radius, he concluded that every second the moon falls toward the earth a distance of 16.1 feet divided by 60×60. Expressed in inches, this is 0.0535, a tiny amount indeed, but an amount that should agree with the observed distance the moon falls toward the earth every second if this theory were correct.

This brought him back to the first task—to figure out from the observed motion of the moon how far it actually falls toward the earth every second. Here Newton called upon his great mathematical skill and his knowledge of the laws of moving bodies. He knew that if a body like the moon is moving in a circle, which he assumed, the distance it falls toward the center of the circle each second can be computed from the radius of the circle and the body's speed. The speed can be calculated from the circumference of the circle and the time it takes the body to revolve once. The general nature of this calculation can be grasped from a fairly simple argument. If the moon were not pulled by the earth, it would move off in a straight line a distance V (its speed) in one second. It would then be farther away from the earth than if it were moving in a circle. To keep on its circle, it then has to fall in a slight amount, which depends on how fast it is moving and on the size of the circle.

In the case of the moon, the radius of the circle is the moon's distance from the earth's center, and the time is the length of the month. Thus Newton had everything he needed to complete the first task. But in doing this calculation, he made a slight error in estimating the radius of the earth; he took it as somewhat smaller than it is. This gave him too small a value for the moon's distance, which he knew to be 60 times the earth's radius. Using this incorrect value for the moon's distance, he found from his calculations that the moon was falling 0.044 inches toward the earth every second.

Not knowing that his estimate of the earth's radius, and hence his calculation of the moon's distance, was wrong, Newton was keenly disappointed in this result, which he accepted as the actual observed value of the distance the moon falls toward the earth every second. It disagreed with his theory, which gave 0.0535 inches, and that to Newton meant that something was wrong with his law of gravity. For six years he put his ideas about gravity aside. In 1671, however, very accurate measurements of the earth's radius were made in France. Newton returned to his calculations, inserting the correct value for the moon's distance. This time everything agreed, and he was jubilant. He was not eager to publish his results but finally did so. As he said, he had found "the force that keeps the moon in her orb" and prevents it from moving off into space along a straight line as it would, owing to its inertia, if there were no such force. From that time on, the name Isaac Newton and the law of gravity have been almost synonymous to people.

Two years after the plague, in the spring of 1667, Newton had returned to Cambridge where his great genius was recognized only slowly. The reason for this was that he was extremely secretive about his thoughts and was very reluctant to talk about his ideas to anyone or to have his discoveries published. In spite of that, he could not hide his brilliance entirely; and in 1668, at the age of twenty-six, he was elected a Fellow of Trinity College. He was awarded a still greater honor a year later when he was appointed Lucasian Professor of Mathematics at Cambridge—one of the highest posts in the world of science. He remained at Cambridge until 1693, continuing his scientific and mathematical studies, which are described in his famous book, *Principia*.

When Newton returned to Cambridge after his two years at Woolsthorpe, he wasn't at all confident about his discoveries. He dreaded proposing anything that might be wrong and thus exposing himself to criticism. He wanted to be absolutely sure that he was right before stating his ideas, and so he spent almost twenty years thinking about the law of gravity and the motions of the planets. Finally, when he could see no error in his reasoning and was firmly convinced by all available evidence that the force of gravity, as he had first perceived it at Woolsthorpe, was correct, he published the theory in his *Principia*.

When he first conceived the law of gravity, he did no more than assure himself that the earth's force of gravity extends not only to the tops of mountains but also to the moon itself. But he quickly saw that there was no reason why it should stop at the moon. He reasoned that it must extend throughout space, growing weaker and weaker at greater and greater distances from the earth, but never vanishing entirely. From that it was but a small step for him to propose the idea that gravity is universal, and that every bit of matter in the universe pulls upon every other bit in accordance with the inverse square law of gravity. These ideas quite naturally led him to the conclusion that the sun pulls the planets and the planets pull the sun.

But he still had to clear up a few things before he could actually calculate how two bodies move when they pull upon each other gravitationally. He had to find precise mathematical equations for the laws of motion, which he did. These state how a body moves when any force acts on it. If no force acts on a body, its inertia keeps it moving with a constant speed in the same straight line. That is its natural tendency (or natural state of motion) from which it departs only when compelled to do so by a force. The larger the force, the less straight is the curve along which the body moves and the more rapidly does its speed change. He then had to find the source of gravity in a body, which he also did. He showed that gravity stems from the mass of a body. The more massive a body is—that is, the more matter it contains—the greater is the gravitational pull it exerts on another given body at a given distance. Thus the sun, being 340,000 times more massive than the earth, exerts 340,000 times as great a gravitational pull on any planet as the earth would if it were at the center of the solar system instead of the sun.

Newton was now prepared for his final great achievement—to show that the gravitational pull of the sun prevents the planets from moving off in straight lines and keeps them, including the earth, in their orbits, compelling each one to move in its own orbit in accordance with Kepler's three laws of planetary motion. With his great mathematical skill and incredible concentration, it didn't take Newton long to deduce Kepler's three laws from his own law of gravitation. This established a far greater harmony and unity than Kepler had, for the law of gravity applies to the whole universe. Each planet in the solar system moves in its own particular orbit (an ellipse of definite size and shape) which was determined entirely by its distance from the sun and its velocity relative to the sun at the time it was born. This can be deduced from the law of gravity. Newton did not publish this remarkable accomplishment at once, as most people would have. Instead, he put the papers on which he had written the mathematical proofs into one of his many drawers and forgot about them.

Some months later, the astronomer Halley, after whom the comet is named, asked Newton if he could deduce Kepler's laws from the law of gravity. Newton said he had already done so, which greatly amazed Halley, who had struggled for months with the problem. But when Newton looked for his mathematical proofs, he could not find them. They were lost! Newton immediately set to work and wrote out the proofs again. He then sent them by messenger to Halley, who prevailed upon Newton to publish this work. Thus began the science that we now call *celestial mechanics*. Without it, space travel and all the feats performed by our astronauts would be impossible, for to send an astronaut to the moon or to place a spacecraft in an orbit around the sun requires the most careful application of the law of gravity. Even a small error in the computation of an orbit can cause a spacecraft to miss its target by millions of miles.

With the completion of his *Principia*, Newton felt that he had accomplished all that he could in science and that the time had come for him to retire and devote himself to such things as alchemy, religion, and philosophy. He had worked very strenuously on the book, neglecting his health and spending more and more time by himself. After the *Principia* was published, he became morose and very strange in his behavior. He wrote rude and often painful letters to his acquaintances, accusing them unjustly of trying to involve him in various affairs that could injure him. To the philosopher John Locke he wrote: "Being of opinion that you endeavor to embroil me with women and by other means, I was so much affected with it . . . that when I was told . . . you were sickly and would not live, I answered, ' 'Twere better if you were dead.' "

For some years Newton's health grew worse, and he finally suffered a nervous breakdown about the time his mother died in 1689. But he recovered fully and spent the last three of his Cambridge years in peace and harmony with others. In 1696 he left Cambridge for London to become Warden of the Mint—a minor governmental post. With that, all his scientific and creative work stopped, and one of the most amazing careers in the history of science ended. He died in Kensington on March 20, 1727, at the age of eighty-four.

Michael had come to the end of his father's manuscript, and he felt somewhat unhappy about it. He felt as though he had been left hanging in the middle of things. What had happened between the time of Newton and the present, he wondered? So much more was known today about the planets than at Newton's death that it couldn't all have been discovered recently. He would talk to his father about it. Michael knew that he would have all his questions answered if he caught his father in the right mood and at the right time. His opportunity came a few days later, on a cold, rainy Saturday.

10·QUESTIONS AND ANSWERS IN THE LIBRARY

When Michael entered the library that rainy Saturday morning after breakfast, his father was just putting aside the daily newspaper.

"Did you find some of the things I wrote difficult to understand?" he asked.

"Not exactly, dad. I understood most of it, and I think I can figure out the rest, but I wonder why you stopped your story with Newton. What about all that happened between Newton's death and the beginning of the twentieth century?"

"Before I answer that question, Michael, I want to clear up the points that puzzled you. What were they?"

"Well, for one thing, if all bodies in the universe pull on one another according to Newton's law, don't the planets also pull on one another?"

"Of course they do, Michael!"

"Well, then, why do they continue moving in elliptical

185

orbits? If they all pull on one another, shouldn't they move in complicated orbits? And shouldn't the sun also be moving because the planets pull on the sun?"

"Two very good points, Michael. The planets actually do move in complicated orbits because they pull on one another. But the gravitational forces of the planets on one another are incredibly small compared to the pull of the sun. The sun, because of its great mass, dominates the solar system and keeps the planets moving in almost elliptical orbits. The planets, by pulling on one another, introduce very small disturbances in the orbits called *perturbations*. These disturbances change the orbits of the planets only slightly over long periods of time. And as far as the sun is concerned, it does indeed move because it is constantly being pulled by the planets. But it moves only very slowly because its mass is enormous. More than 99 percent of the entire mass of the solar system is concentrated in the sun, making it very sluggish compared to the planets. Because the sun is so sluggish, the planets have only a tiny effect on it."

"But what about the stars outside the solar system, dad? Don't they pull on the planets and change their orbits?"

"Hardly at all, Michael. The closest star is so far away from us that its gravitational attraction on any planet is about a billion times smaller than the sun's attraction. The nearby stars have an effect on comets, though. We believe today that there are about two hundred billion comets forming a halo around the solar system, halfway between our sun and the nearest star. Most of the comets just stay out there, going around the sun once every forty or fifty million years. But every now and then the gravitational pull of the nearby stars, small as it is, slows one of the comets down, causing it to fall in toward the sun. We then see it moving in an elongated orbit around the sun."

"Is that the only gravitational effect the stars have on our solar system?"

"No. There is one other important gravitational effect which the stars that form the Milky Way have on each other. The Milky Way, as was first discovered by Galileo, is a vast galaxy of more than a hundred billion stars, with most of the stars concentrated in a huge core. Our sun, which lies outside the core, is but one of these billions of stars. Just as the planets in our solar system revolve around the sun because of the sun's gravitational pull, so our entire solar system revolves around the core of the Milky Way once every two hundred and fifty million years because of the gravitational pull of the core. We are so far away from the center of this core that it takes light from it thirty thousand years to reach us. Because of this great distance, the gravitational pull of the galactic core on our solar system is about one hundred times smaller than the gravitational pull of the sun on the earth. This force, which is about equal to the weight of the entire earth, keeps our solar system moving in a vast circle around the galaxy, at a speed of about one hundred and forty miles per second."

Michael thought about these things for a few minutes without saying anything, while his father looked at him questioningly.

"I followed most of what you said, dad. It is just that to go from the solar system to the galaxy is such an enormous step that I just had to stop and think about it for a moment. I wonder what Kepler, Galileo, and Newton would say about all the knowledge we now have."

"I don't think they would be too surprised. Some people were ready to accept such ideas in Kepler's time, and Giordano Bruno was burned at the stake in 1601 for proposing the idea that each star is a sun with its own planets. But the knowledge we have now didn't come easily. Most of what we know about stars and galaxies was discovered within the last sixty years."

"Do you mean that not very much was discovered from the time of Newton's death to the beginning of the twentieth century?"

"Many things were discovered then, Michael, but the great discoveries in astronomy had to wait until large, accurate telescopes could be built, and that didn't happen until the present century. But that doesn't mean important astronomical work wasn't being done. Once Newton introduced the law of gravity and calculus, the great mathematicians who followed him developed very beautiful and complex mathematical methods for solving gravitational problems of all kinds and for checking Newton's law."

"But why was that necessary, dad? I thought Newton had proved his law by testing it against the moon's motion."

"That was not a good enough proof because the moon is pulled not only by the earth but also by all the other bodies in the solar system. That is the beauty of Newton's law, for it shows the great harmony in the universe with all bodies pulling upon one another and thus keeping the whole thing going. To prove Newton's law precisely, we have to take into account all the bodies pulling on the moon. That's a very difficult problem—too difficult even for Newton. Special mathematical methods were needed, and that is why the great mathematicians after Newton worked on this problem for many years. By the middle of the nineteenth century, enough mathematical work had been done on the motions of planets, taking into account the pull of the planets on themselves, to show that Newton's law was very accurate. And yet there was one little flaw. Mercury did not quite obey the law. It was found that Mercury departed from its predicted position by a very tiny amount every hundred years."

"Did that mean that Newton's law was wrong?"

"Yes. But it wasn't wrong by much."

"Then what happened?"

"Very little for more than another half century. Then Einstein came along with his law of gravity, and the problem of Mercury's motion was solved."

"I'd love to hear about that. That's the general theory of relativity, isn't it?"

"Yes but we can't go into that now. It's much too complicated, and the mathematics required to understand it are beyond you right now."

"Well then, what about Venus? We must know a great deal more about it today than Newton knew."

"From relativity to Venus. You do jump around, Michael."

"Well, you remember, dad, this whole thing began with a question about Venus. It seems that nothing much more was known about Venus at Newton's time than at the time of Aristarchus. What about today?"

"Oh, we know a great deal more about it now than Newton or the astronomers of the eighteenth and nineteenth centuries did. But we discovered most of the interesting things about Venus only recently. Even the large optical telescopes like those at Mount Wilson and Palomar revealed very little about the planet. The reason is that Venus is completely surrounded by thick white clouds that completely hide its surface from us. Just as we cannot see the sun, moon, or stars when our skies are cloudy, so we cannot look through the clouds on Venus."

"Were these clouds discovered recently?"

"No. Astronomers have known about them for some time. The clouds are white—the same color as the ordinary clouds in our sky. That is one reason Venus appears so bright. Its clouds reflect a great deal of the sunlight that strikes the planet. The strange thing about these clouds is that, in spite of all our efforts, we still don't know their chemical nature. But even with these clouds, we have learned a great deal about Venus, and some of it is quite amazing."

"You mean astronomers have ways of looking through the clouds? They can use a certain kind of radiation that passes right through the clouds. Is that it?"

"Yes, Michael, but before I come to that, I'll tell you how much astronomers learned about Venus before they penetrated the clouds. Such things as its size, its mass, its density and the length of its year can be measured or calculated in spite of the clouds. The length of Venus's year is 224.7 earth days. It is shorter than the earth's year because Venus is 67 million miles from the sun whereas the earth's distance from the sun is 93 million miles. The orbit of Venus is thus about 30 percent shorter than the earth's orbit, and also, the sun pulls harder on Venus than it does on the earth, making Venus move faster. Because Venus is about 30 percent closer to the sun than we are, it receives about 90 percent more light and heat from the sun than we do."

"But how do you find the mass of Venus? That seems quite difficult."

"It isn't very difficult, but it is harder than finding the mass of a planet like Jupiter that has moons. We could find the mass of Venus if it had a moon by applying Newton's law of gravity to the motion of the moon. Since Venus has no moon, astronomers found its mass by observing how its gravitational pull, which depends on its mass, changes the orbit of a comet that comes close to it.

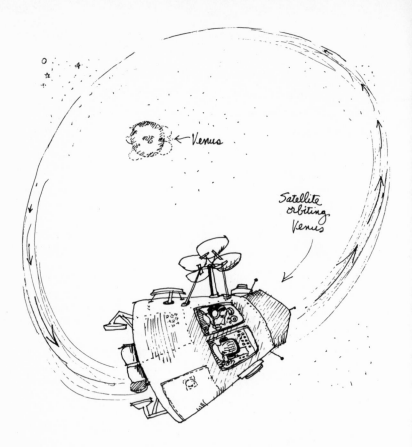

Venus

Satellite orbiting Venus

We can determine the mass of Venus by placing an artificial satellite in orbit around it at a definite distance and then accurately measuring the time it takes the satellite to revolve around Venus once. From this number and the distance of the satellite from the center of Venus, the mass of Venus can be found using Newton's law of gravity. The density of Venus can be obtained by dividing its mass by its total volume (the volume of a sphere having a radius equal to Venus' radius).

Today it is even easier than that. We send a spacecraft past Venus, as the Russians and Americans have already done, and observe the gravitational pull of Venus on this craft. That, combined with Newton's law of gravity, gives us the mass of Venus, which is about 82 percent of the earth's mass. Its diameter, which can be calculated since its apparent size (its angular size) and its distance from the earth is known, is 7560 miles. The density of Venus—how compact it is (the mass in a unit volume)—can be calculated from its mass and its diameter. One divides its total mass by its total volume. It is about as compact as the earth is."

"But what good is all that if you can't see the surface and find out what's really going on there, dad?"

"Just from what I have told you, astronomers have deduced a great deal about Venus. From its size, mass, and compactness we know that its structure is about the same as the earth's and that it is composed of a mixture of iron, nickel, and rocky materials. The iron and nickel are probably at the center of Venus in the form of a hot liquid, just as they are at the center of the earth."

"Does that mean that the surface of Venus is something like the earth's surface?"

"Yes, it does. There are mountain peaks, valleys, and vast plains on Venus, just as there are on the earth. In a moment I'll tell you how astronomers discovered all of that, in spite of the clouds. This is recent knowledge, but even before direct evidence showed that the surface features on Venus and the earth are similar, scientists suspected this was so. That led many people to believe

An observer on the earth measures the diameter of Venus by first measuring the angle of Venus' diameter as observed on the earth and then multiplying this diameter by the distance of Venus from the earth.

Venus

Diameter of Venus

angle of Venus' diameter as seen from the earth

that Venus was habitable, and that beneath its cloud lay vast oceans, forests, rivers, and lakes, just as on the earth. They didn't stop there but pictured the forests teeming with the most incredible kinds of plants and animals. You recall the early science-fiction writers—authors like Edgar Rice Burroughs—who wrote stories about vast cities on Venus with beautiful princesses always being rescued by earthlings who somehow or other found themselves on Venus."

"I've read some, dad. They were terrific. But wouldn't the clouds that surround Venus prevent it from warming up? How do the sun's rays get through the clouds?"

"The clouds are not solid structures. They consist of small particles of some kind or other, just as our clouds consist of small particles of water. Such a collection of particles reflects ordinary light extremely well, but some light gets through. That's why it is fairly bright on the earth even on a very cloudy day. The clouds surrounding Venus reflect about 80 percent of the sunlight and allow 20 percent of it to get through and strike the surface of Venus. Since Venus, being nearer to the sun, receives almost twice as much radiation from the sun as we do every second, 20 percent of that would be enough to give Venus an average temperature slightly higher than the earth's. The clouds contribute to this by reflecting back onto Venus most of the radiation reflected from its surface. Almost every bit of the solar radiation hitting the surface of Venus thus helps increase its temperature. People were quite sure that the climate on Venus was something like the climate in subtropical regions on the earth."

"But what about the rotation of Venus? Doesn't that affect its climate, dad?"

"Yes, it does. To see how rotation affects climate, let's consider the earth for a moment. If the earth rotated on its axis once a year, one hemisphere of the earth would always face the sun and be in perpetual daylight, while the other would always face away from the sun and be in constant darkness. It would then always be extremely hot on the bright side of the earth and very, very cold on the other side. The circulation of the atmosphere would tend to even things out a bit, but it wouldn't change things much. The tilt of the earth's axis of rotation—the angle the earth's axis makes with a line to the sun—is also important. If that angle were 90 degrees instead of 66.5 degrees, the climate on the earth would never change. In the temperate zones we would always have balmy, springlike weather."

"But how do astronomers measure the rotation of Venus if it's covered with clouds?"

"In fact, for a long time astronomers could not determine its rate of rotation because they could see no surface markings like those on Mars to guide them. But there is a way of measuring the rotation by using the spectroscope, an instrument that breaks light up into its colors. If a planet is spinning, the light coming to us from the edge of the planet that is moving away from us is somewhat redder than the light from the center of the planet, and the light coming from the edge approaching us is somewhat bluer. This behavior of light is called the *Doppler effect* because it was discovered in 1842 by the

Austrian physicist Christian Doppler. By measuring this effect for a planet (that is, by noting the difference in color from one edge of the planet to the other), we can determine the speed of its rotation.

"When astronomers examined the light from the two edges of Venus with a spectroscope, they found no measurable Doppler effect. This meant that if Venus was rotating at all, it was doing so too slowly to show a measurable Doppler effect. Some astronomers believed that it rotated only once every 225.6 days, always keeping the same face toward the sun. But that idea ran into some trouble because measurements of the heat radiated from the dark side of Venus—the side away from the sun—showed that it was much warmer than it ought to be if it never received any sunlight at all, as would be the case if Venus always kept one face to the sun."

"Do we know much more about it today?"

"Yes indeed, Michael. During the last few years astronomers have studied the surface of Venus with radar beams. Such beams pass right through the clouds on Venus and are reflected back to us from its surface. When they return to us from the surface of Venus, they show a definite and measurable Doppler effect which varies with the part of the surface from which these beams were reflected. From such radar echoes astronomers have found that Venus rotates on its axis once every 243 days. This means that it does not keep the same face to the sun and its day is longer than its year. But now comes the really interesting part about this business, which we did not know before. We now know that Venus rotates in the opposite direction from the earth—opposite from the direction in which it revolves around the sun. If you were on Venus and could see the sky, the sun and the stars would all rise in the west and set in the east."

"But, dad, how did that come about? Venus is so similar to the earth and so close to it that one would expect it to behave very nearly like the earth."

"Yes, but it is closer to the sun, and that makes all the difference. Even though Venus is only about 30 percent closer to the sun than we are, the tidal action of the gravitational field of the sun on Venus is about 3.5 times as great as it is on the earth. When Venus was first formed as a planet, it probably was spinning as fast as the earth, and it probably was also in a molten state. The large tides raised on its molten surface by the pull of the sun slowed it down after billions of years until it was spinning at the same rate as it was revolving. At that time Venus kept the same face toward the sun. But then, whenever Venus came closest to the earth, the earth by its tidal action slowed down the rotation of Venus still more and finally caused it to rotate in the opposite direction. Now everything is in equilibrium. We are not completely sure that it all came about this way, but it's a reasonable explanation."

"What about the present conditions on Venus, dad? How do we know that its surface is as hot as they say?"

"It took a long time to discover that, again, because of those dense clouds surrounding Venus. It is, indeed, the most mysterious of all the planets, but more than forty years ago astronomers began to suspect that the conditions on Venus might be quite different from those on earth because they found the chemistry of Venus's atmosphere to be quite different from the earth's. Using the spectroscope, they detected a great deal of carbon dioxide—much more than in the earth's atmosphere— and hardly any oxygen or water vapor. From the presence of so much carbon dioxide in the atmosphere of Venus, astronomers reasoned that its surface might be quite warm with a temperature of at least 100 degrees Centigrade because carbon dioxide doesn't let very much heat escape from the planet. It absorbs the heat rays. These results were quite disappointing to people who thought there was life on Venus. But they still didn't give up their hope that life might be there because they felt that the spectroscope couldn't really tell us what's going on below the clouds."

"What happened then?"

"Radio astronomers came on the scene and dashed all hopes for life on Venus. Radio waves, like those that you receive on your AM or FM set or your television, and light are both examples of electromagnetic radiation, which is sent out by electric charges that are moving about in a helter-skelter way. If such charges are dashing around at about one-hundredth the speed of light, as they are inside excited atoms, they send out mostly light. We may think of the eye, then, as a tiny radiation receiver that responds only to the kind of radiation that we call light. If electric charges—also called *ions*—are dashing about at much smaller speeds, they emit mostly radio waves. The hotter the material is that contains the electric charges, the faster the electric charges dash about, and the greater is the total amount of radiation of all kinds they emit.

"Using the basic laws of radiation, scientists have discovered simple formulas which show how the quality and intensity of the radiation emitted by a hot object are related to its temperature. Now, about fifteen years ago, radio astronomers, using large radio telescopes, picked up radio waves from Venus. The intensity of these radio waves showed, in accordance with the laws I mentioned, that the surface temperature of Venus is about 800 degrees Farenheit—much too hot for any kind of life."

"But that is still indirect evidence, dad. How can we be sure that the radiation laws apply to radio waves from Venus?"

"There can be no question about that. But if you're unhappy with what you call indirect evidence, I can give you direct evidence which you know about because you were very excited about it when the evidence was gathered."

"You mean the Russian Venera series and the U.S. Mariner series of spacecraft that reached Venus and sent back information about its surface and atmosphere?"

"Yes, Michael. The Mariner spacecraft passed right through the atmosphere of Venus and sent back signals to us that had to pass back through Venus's atmosphere before reaching us. The Venera series sent up by the Russians were landing craft that dropped through the atmosphere of Venus and were designed to land on its surface. The first two of these landing spacecraft stopped sending back information when they were only partway through the atmosphere. They were probably destroyed by the intense heat and other severe conditions before they landed. But the third Russian Venera flight was successful. The craft landed in 1970 on the surface of Venus and continued sending back information for about twenty-three minutes after landing. The data received from the U.S. and Russian spacecrafts left no doubt about the conditions on Venus. The surface of the planet is extremely hot, hot enough to melt lead, and the atmospheric pressure is one ton per square inch, about one hundred and thirty times as large as the pressure at sea level here on the earth. That follows directly from the very high surface temperature. It equals the pressure you would experience if you sank to a depth of three thousand feet in the ocean."

"What about the atmosphere of Venus and the cloud surrounding it? Did the spacecraft tell us anything about these?"

"Yes, Michael, a great deal. Not so much about the cloud but about the atmosphere. The Russian craft had no trouble measuring the amount of carbon dioxide in the atmosphere, and confirmed what we had already suspected when the radio waves from Venus indicated that the surface was very hot. From the Russian spacecraft we now know quite definitely that 95 percent of the atmosphere is carbon dioxide and that small quantities of oxygen and water vapor are also present. If all the water vapor on Venus were condensed, there would be enough liquid to cover the surface of Venus to a depth of one foot, which is a tiny amount. If all the water here were spread out equally over the entire earth, every point on the earth's surface would lie beneath eight thousand feet of water. An interesting question which arises is where did Venus's water go? We'll come back to that.

"We may now be able to explain the cloud surrounding Venus. Because of the very high atmospheric pressure and high temperature, the winds on Venus rush around at hundreds of miles per hour, raising vast sandstorms that drive clouds of sand many hundreds of miles into the atmosphere. These tiny particles of sand, dredged up by powerful winds from the very dry surface of Venus, form the clouds that surround the planet."

"Does carbon dioxide in the atmosphere of Venus account for its high temperature?"

"Yes, as I have already told you. When carbon dioxide was first discovered in the atmosphere of Venus, astronomers knew that it would cause what we call the *greenhouse effect.* Carbon dioxide allows sunlight to get down to the surface of Venus, but it blocks most of the infrared rays emitted by Venus when Venus warms up. Carbon dioxide makes an atmosphere behave like a one-way street for light and heat. Light from the sun can get in, but heat from the planet can't get out. The planet thus gets hotter and hotter until, finally, it is so hot that enough of its heat, in fact, only a small amount, gets out to keep everything steady but at a very high temperature."

"Well, everything about Venus seems pretty clear now

except one thing, dad. Why is there so little oxygen and water on Venus and so much carbon dioxide?"

"We have an answer to that also, Michael, but some of it involves some complicated chemistry and knowledge about the conditions on the earth and Venus when they were first formed as planets. It is probable that the present atmospheres on the earth and Venus are quite different from the original atmospheres on these planets. Venus and earth lost their original atmospheres and existed for some time as dry, lifeless bodies. Then vast volcanoes erupted on both planets sending out huge gaseous clouds of nitrogen, carbon dioxide, and water vapor. On the earth the temperature was just right, owing to its distance from the sun, to allow the cool rocks of the earth's crust to absorb most of the carbon dioxide—all but a few hundredths of a percent. But not so for Venus. It was too close to the sun for its rocks to be cool enough to absorb its vast amount of carbon dioxide. So, as more and more carbon dioxide accumulated, the surface of Venus grew hotter and hotter, resulting in an even greater concentration of carbon dioxide, and so on. There was thus a runaway 'greenhouse effect.'"

"But what about the water on Venus? Where did it go?"

"The sun's ultraviolet rays broke up the water molecules into hydrogen and oxygen, and the hydrogen atoms escaped from Venus. That didn't happen on the earth because the earth was, and still is, surrounded by an ozone layer that traps the sun's ultraviolet rays and so protects our water supply. Ozone is a molecule of oxygen containing three oxygen atoms. Without ozone, there could be no water; and without water, life couldn't begin on Venus; and without life, there could be no oxygen. You see now that things all fall neatly into place."

"Do you think astronauts will ever land on Venus and explore it the way they did the moon, dad?"

"Probably, but not for some time. If an astronaut could land on Venus and survive, he would see the most weird landscape and sky imaginable. If dense dust storms were always present, he would have great difficulty in seeing anything at all. But if there were no dust storms, the extremely dense atmosphere would greatly distort the appearance of the sky and the horizon by bending the sun's rays. The light from the sun would be bent to such an extent on passing through the Venus atmosphere that the astronaut could still see the sun rise or set even if he turned his back to it. It would be like looking into a mirror. Moreover, if the astronaut could see the rising or setting sun at all, he would not see it as a disk but as a many-colored band along the horizon."

Michael looked out the window of the library as his father finished talking. The rain had stopped. The sun was breaking through the clouds, and, just as on that day a few weeks ago, its rays again cast a warm glow over the bookshelves. All the books were still there with their mysterious titles, and they beckoned him even more now than they had then. But now they seemed less forbidding and difficult, and he knew that he would master them in time. The authors had not been supermen. They had all been boys like him at one time, trying to understand the world around them and struggling with problems just as he was now.

He was confident that he would become a scientist and do good scientific work. There were hundreds of problems to be solved, and he would help solve them. Perhaps not the way Newton and Einstein did, but in a way that would satisfy him and give him pleasure. He recalled something that Newton had said, "If I have seen farther than others, it was because I stood on the shoulders of giants." But he, Michael, had the shoulders of many more giants to stand on than Newton had.

Suddenly he felt very happy.